Realistic
Bug Out Bag
Max Cooper

Realistic Bug Out Bag

Reproduction or translation of any part of this work beyond that permitted by section 107 or 108 of the 1976 United States Copyright Act without permission of the copyright owner is unlawful. The author believes, to the best of his knowledge, that the information provide in this book is correct at the time of this writing.

DISCLAIMER AND/OR LEGAL NOTICES:

Care has been taken to confirm the accuracy of the information presented. However, the author and publisher are not responsible for errors or omissions or for any consequences from application of the information in this book and make no warranty, expressed or implied, with respect to the currency, completeness, or accuracy of the contents of the publication. The content provided is for entertainment purposes only.

Copyright © 2014 Max Cooper
All Rights Reserved
ISBN-13: 978-1499215076
ISBN-10: 149921507X

Table of Contents

Introduction 1
Kit Methodology 16
Bug Out Bag Assessment 27
Fire 48
Water 53
Food 64
Shelter 69
Light 75
Communications 79
Clothing 93
Medical 99
Weapons 107
Pets 114
Miscellaneous Items 118
Summary 150
Resources 156
References 170

Realistic Bug Out Bag

There are no guarantees during a bug out event.

Train hard;

pack light;

have a plan;

be prepared.

Max Cooper

Introduction

The world of bug out bags can be overwhelming, frustrating, and overcomplicated. It does not have to be this way. Everyone is looking to create a name, acronym, or mnemonic to come up with a different way of saying the same thing. I'm going to keep things simple and call a bug out bag a bug out bag! When it comes to bug out bags everyone has an opinion and there is no lack of resources on the matter. Unfortunately, a lot of the information presented is by people who have never bugged out, never had to walk ten to twenty miles with their pack, and have never tested their set-up. They have never felt the weight of a heavy pack on their shoulders. They have not felt the agony of blisters on their feet or the hot sun on their skin for hours at a time. Even if you plan to bug out with a vehicle you must have a contingency plan that requires you to walk with your pack for an extended distance. There is a world of difference between creating a long list of what should go in your bug out bag verse having to bug out for a real situation. Yet, these people feel confident dictating what you should carry with the belief that the more you have the more you are prepared. Much of this information is simply: WRONG!

Realistic Bug Out Bag

It is wrong for two significant reasons:

1. They recommend you carry too much gear
2. The total weight will be too heavy to carry for most people

Too much gear and too much weight come with a very high cost. These reasons should not be overlooked or minimized. Bugging out does not mean that you fill your bag until the zippers are about to break. All this gear means that your pack is going to be too heavy to effectively negotiate a bug out. Sometimes **less is more** especially when you have to carry your pack and potentially walk for an unknown distance. The reality is that most people are not in the best physical conditioning. Even if you are just 20 pounds overweight you are going to feel it when bugging out on foot. Do not have the belief that you are just going to put your pack on your back and forge on for miles upon miles. This is unrealistic wishful thinking that will result in dire consequences. More often than not, most people that I have talked with who have a bug out bag ready to go have never even worn the pack outside of their house! They have not tested their bag, gear, set-up, or themselves. It is during a crisis they are going to find out that their pack is too heavy or hurts their back or shoulders. They will quickly learn the hot spots, pain, and frustration that lack of preparedness brings to the forefront. They will be sucking in air as they pathetically struggle to keep going. At this point it is too late and you have failed yourself and potentially your family. Putting together a bug out bag is a process and is not just about putting a bunch of survival gear in a backpack. You are going to have to be able to carry your pack for an unknown distance, possibly during inclement weather, and potentially facing people with harmful intentions toward you and your family. Having a lifestyle that includes eating healthy, exercising, not smoking, and using alcohol moderately will matter when it comes time to hit the road.

The other realization that people tend to overlook is that bugging out is NOT a comfortable situation. It will be due to an 'event' that will take you out of your comfort zone and it is generally very stressful. Even if you believe that you are well prepared you will still be impacted by stress. Additionally, something always goes wrong which will mess up your plans. It is important that you do not over pack your bug out bag to try and recreate the comforts of home. You must accept the fact that you will be uncomfortable and will not be able to take all the "wants" that you had pre-crisis. It is best to stick to the priorities that will keep you alive. These are your "**needs**." This is not to say you can't take a "want" with you but you must choose very wisely and keep it to an absolute minimum.

Realistic Bug Out Bag

Many people have their bug out bag set up for 72 hours or three days which is a good period of time to be prepared. Those who have their bag set up for longer time periods tend to over pack and are then stuck with a heavy load. If you are in peak physical conditioning and can handle the load then go for it. Also, do not assume that because you were in the military 15 years ago and did a lot of marching or combat missions that you are still capable of the same feats now. I am focusing on the "average" person who is not in great shape. For these people a 72 hour kit is good provided that they focus on needs; not wants. Always keep in mind that every additional item that you add to your bag has a weight requirement attached to it that you must be able to carry.

The best way to test your kit and your conditioning is to go for a 10 mile hike with your bug out bag. If you have never done this exercise you will learn a lot about what to do, what not to do, and modifications that you need to make. After your modifications are implemented take another 10 mile hike and re-evaluate your kit. Once you get to the point where you think your kit is good to go it is then time to take a 15 mile hike. Go back and modify your set up if needed. Then take a 20 mile hike. At this point you will be able to fine tune your set up and make necessary changes. After this exercise is completed you will have a pack that weighs what it needs to weigh because you will eliminate all of the excess gear that is not absolutely required. It is amazing the decisions you will make about your bug out bag when your lungs are on fire as you struggle to get necessary oxygen into your bloodstream, your back hurts, and you have blisters on your feet. If you decide to skip this exercise I can guarantee that you will not be prepared. Until you walk twenty miles with your pack and feel the weight on your shoulders you will not truly understand the importance of this exercise. It is the only way to know what you are capable of carrying.

This book is about providing information. It is not about whether you agree or disagree with the presented ideas. **Take what is useful to you and discard the rest.** Arguing over such points is valueless and does not add to your situation. Do not get sucked into arguments about minutia that is not that important. Instead, spend your time wisely and remain focused on your overall preparedness goals. Therefore, this book is not about lists although lists are included. It is about getting you to think about the pros and cons of the equipment that you choose to carry. It is about getting you to understand the cost/benefit ratio of every ounce you choose to carry. Not everything that you may need in your bug out bag will be listed in this book because only you will know how to decide what the contents of your bag should be based on your individual needs. There are just too many variables that will dictate what you should carry in your bug out bag.

Realistic Bug Out Bag

These variables include:

Type of bug out incident

Natural Disasters – Hurricane, tornado, flood, earthquake, tsunami, landslide, volcano, wildfire, severe dust storm, extreme heat or cold.

Terrorism – Chemical, Biological, Radiological, Nuclear, Explosive (CBRNE), active shooter, improvised explosive device (IED), simultaneous multiple terrorist events, attack on the power grid - water supply - mass transportation, etc.

Civil Unrest – Could be due to political factors, economic crisis, isolated local incident, societal breakdown, low intensity conflict, war, etc.

Variables

- *Age* - The reality is that as you age things can become more challenging. You may have medical conditions that limits your capabilities, you may be more prone to injuries, and your senses may not be as acute such as vision, hearing, and sense of smell.

- Location – Urban, Suburban, or rural environment. Your location will be a huge factor in determining the contents of your bug out bag.

- Weather and Environmental Factors - Heat, cold, humidity, snow, rain, dust, decreased visibility, day time, night time, smoke conditions, fire, crowds, blocked access to areas, barriers such as water, fences, walls, etc.

- Elevation – Altitude increases oxygen requirements.

- Physical Fitness Level - To include strength and endurance.

- Your Knowledge-Skills-Abilities: A wide variety of skills may be necessary during a crisis. Your background and experience may come in handy such as: Military, law enforcement, firefighter, first responder, doctor, paramedic, nurse, EMT, mechanic, electrician, etc.

- Members - Who is with you such as young children or elderly parents? How many people in your group is another factor as there may be safety in numbers. Keep in mind that the more people who are with you the slower you will generally tend to move.

- Violence Potential – Individual acts of random violence, mobs, street gangs, riot, civil unrest, societal breakdown, and war.

- Public Safety Resources - Police, fire, medical, hospitals, and other emergency services.

- Medical Conditions - Heart problems, diabetes, seizures, asthma, or current injury such as a sprain, strain, or fracture. Impaired vision or decreased hearing ability. Conditions that require medication on a regular basis.

- Mental Health Status - Depression, anxiety or other conditions that may impact your ability to handle stress and the unknown. Lack of a support system or inability to reach needed services such as a counselor, therapist, or support group.

It is impossible for any book to cover each variable. This is why it is going to be critical for you to know and understand your strengths, weaknesses, and the particulars of your situation. You will not find that in a book as it is uniquely individualized to you. It is also important to understand some of the realities of a bug out situation.

When faced with a bug out you should automatically make some assumptions that are based on past experience from prior incidents. Assumptions are generally bad but **the best predictor of future behavior is past behavior.** These scenarios have been repeated time and time again in the United States and throughout the world. You would be wise to think about the following situations and how to incorporate plans to deal with each one.

In a bug out situation assume that:

- Evacuation routes are going to be jam packed with traffic that severely limits your ability to travel in a timely manner. Traffic can potentially become so bad that you get stuck in gridlock. Additionally, when people get stuck in traffic they tend to become frustrated, angry, and potentially violent. When you are stuck in gridlock you also become a static target for predators who may attempt to take advantage of the situation. What will you do in this situation?

- Resources such as food, water, and fuel will quickly be consumed potentially leaving you in a situation where none is available. Grocery stores, convenience stores, and gas stations will quickly run out of needed resources. What will you do if your vehicle runs out of fuel before you reach your destination?

- Sanitation can quickly become a problem leading to illness which can severely limit or completely end your ability to bug out. What then?

- Violence can be a significant problem in the forms of rioting, looting, and interpersonal violence from individuals, groups, or gangs. Are you capable of protecting yourself and your family?

If you take away anything from this book I want you to understand that you must test yourself and your equipment. Unfortunately, too many people are:

1. Lazy and will not take the time to test themselves, or

2. They inaccurately believe that theirs skills and physical conditioning is better than it really is

It is you and your family that will pay the price if you fail to test your gear and yourself.

This step cannot be skipped.

Remember, most people over pack their bug out bag and think they are good to go. If you do not put some miles on the ground by walking with your bug out bag on your back you will be in for a shocker during a real bug out event. This test will tell you if your pack is too heavy and your level of physical fitness. When you identify problems you must then develop a plan to fix the problems and then conduct another test. This will need to be repeated until you have all of the kinks worked out. This will also have the added benefit of drastically increasing your confidence during a real situation because you have taken the time to test your plans, your kit and yourself.

If your physical fitness is an issue you will need to write down some very specific goals to get in shape so that you are capable of effectively bugging out with your pack. I am a big proponent of goal setting and highly recommend that you learn and implement goal setting skills. A good resource for goal setting is a book called "**How to Set Goals and Keep Them: S.M.A.R.T. Goals**" by Scott Kirshner, M.Ed.[i]

I like this book because it is short and provides a fail-safe method of writing goals. If you follow the method outlined in the book you will be able to write very detailed and specific goals so that you know your responsibility for successful goal obtainment.

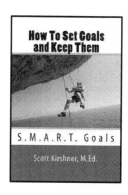

Realistic Bug Out Bag

When it comes to emergency preparedness it is critical to write your goals down so that you are following a specific program and not skipping anything. The ability to write down your goals is a valuable skill to know and even better to implement.

If you take the time to test your gear and yourself you will be better prepared than 95% of preppers. Unfortunately, too many people skip this part and are not as prepared as they believe. They are only fooling themselves. But, your dark secret will come to see the full light of day when it comes time to bug out and you are dead tired after walking only one mile with your bug out bag on your back. It is at that point you will have wished you had properly prepared. A little self-reflection and honesty in evaluating your capabilities and your weaknesses will allow you to make necessary changes. These changes will require effort, consistency, discipline, and determination on your part to implement so that your identified weaknesses are eliminated. The result will be an increased level of calm, confidence, physical ability, and preparedness. This will translate to peace of mind on the day you need to bug out for real. Once you get to this point you will need to have a plan and written goals to maintain your achievements so that you do not slip back into old habits that lead to unpreparedness. It becomes a "lifestyle" and not a short term goal that is attained and then quickly lost.

Max Cooper

Best Case Scenario vs. Worst Case Scenario

I have always considered myself a lifelong student. I like learning new skills and refining old ones. I enjoy learning more effective ways to accomplish tasks. I constantly seek out new training opportunities that will improve my skillset and knowledge. Sometimes I walk out of a class learning what not to do which is beneficial as well. I have trained with many different trainers and sought out and paid for many training classes. It does not take me long to figure out if an instructor knows what they are talking about or if they are going through the paces and regurgitating information that someone told them without having any true understanding or insight on the material being presented. I highly encourage you to seek out training classes that will fill in the knowledge gaps that you are missing.

Far too many training classes focus on what I call the *"Best Case Scenario"* model. This is training where the outcome is always positive, the students always succeed, and everyone walks out of the class feeling confident but without acquiring any new skills. This is bad and provides students who do not perform well a false level of confidence. This is not benefiting anyone but the instructor or training company that is putting on the training. All students get praised whether they performed well or horribly. It is done for numerous reasons: the instructor doesn't have the necessary training skills, the instructor does not want

Realistic Bug Out Bag

to hurt anyone's feelings, the instructor doesn't want to offend anyone, or the training company is striving to get your hard earned money to attend another class. This is wrong and unethical. Training should be preparing people for the "**Worst Case Scenario**." Students who can handle the worst case scenario are surly prepared to handle the best case scenario. The opposite rarely is the case. Training classes should be challenging, provide new skills, and provide feedback that is accurate and helpful. Students who perform poorly should not be ridiculed but provided additional instruction for improvement so they walk away from the class with specific skills to work on and improve. This builds confidence through hard work and challenging training. Students should be presented with scenarios that can be solved so they are not set up to fail. Classes that you may consider attending, based on your needs, include:

- Firearms marksmanship
- Firearms tactics
- Team tactics
- Urban survival
- Wilderness survival
- Medical training
- Search and rescue
- Rappelling
- Communications skills

- Desert survival
- Arctic survival
- Escape and evasion
- Camouflage skills
- Shelter building skills
- Hunting and fishing
- Wild edible training
- Gear training and packing
- Physical fitness and nutrition
- Primitive skills (last resort)

The list can go on and on depending on your needs. Identify a weakness and then look for a class to learn and develop the necessary skill.

It can be challenging to find quality classes with great instructors but when you do you hit the jackpot. You will leave with new skills, insights, and confidence. You will be willing to spend your hard earned money for more classes. If you attend a class that was not beneficial you have some options to address this problem. You can talk to the instructor in a polite and professional manner and state where the class fell short along with suggestions for improvement. If you do not want to do this most classes will have you complete a course evaluation where you can provide this information.

Realistic Bug Out Bag

Kit Methodology

At the heart of every bug out bag should be a core set of items that you carry regardless of the event or emergency. From there you can add specific items based on individual needs such as environmental factors or medical conditions. You may also have to modify your set up based upon the specific situation that you are preparing your kit. The methodology of designing your kit should be designed around surviving for 72 hours and then adding items based on specific situations that you may encounter. The main part of your kit should be considered your "core kit" and with this kit you should be able to go most places in the world and survive 72 hours. These items are the foundation of your kit and are required regardless of what event you are preparing. Always begin building your kit with a strong foundation of essential items, known as needs, and then adding on items based on other factors. Too many people get focused on "other factors" and then lose sight of the core components.

It is also important to obtain your core components before buying your pack. **It should be the contents that determine the pack and not the pack that determines the contents.** Too often the novice will buy a pack to *fill* with gear instead of purchasing a pack to *hold* your gear. With the vast variety of packs available you should have no problem finding a pack to suit your needs. If you have specific requirements you can have your bag modified.

Generally, it is recommended that you utilize a high quality backpack that has the following:

- Place for a 100 ounce hydration bladder
- Padded shoulder straps
- Vented back
- Chest strap to help with stabilization
- Waist belt to help with stabilization
- Heavy duty YKK zippers with paracord zipper pulls
- Double stitching especially at stress points
- MOLLE webbing for attaching items
- Quality buckles that will not easily break
- Triple polyurethane coated for water resistance
- High tensile strength composite nylon thread which is stronger than ordinary industry standard nylon thread

Realistic Bug Out Bag

Pack aspects that you may want to avoid include:

- A lot of people like packs that use 1000-Denier material which is very strong. But this material tends to be very stiff. You can get a backpack that is not 1000-Denier that will be strong enough for all of your needs. If you decide to use 1000-Denier that is fine just realize it is very stiff. It is very high quality material and you may find that it fits your needs especially if you are in a harsh environment with a lot of thorns.

- Avoid reflective material that is built into the backpack which is especially if you are trying to be low key in a low-light environment. If I want reflective material on my pack I want to be the one to be able to put it on and take it off.

- Stay away from single shoulder straps as they lead to shoulder fatigue and do not hold much gear. A single shoulder strap should not be an option for you. I have even gotten away from single shoulder straps for my everyday carry (EDC) bag. I tried it for a year but it just does not work for me.

- Avoid bright colored packs that will draw attention to you. Stick with neutral colors or colors that help you blend into your environment.

DO NOT STICK OUT; BLEND IN. (Maybe!)

A Different Approach:

The style of pack that you decide to use is a controversial topic. Essentially there are two ways to go: Non-descript and military looking. Again, there is no right or wrong there are only pros and cons based on your situation.

Non-Descript

The thought with the non-descript bag is that you will not stand out and people will leave you alone. Your goal is to blend into your environment and not look like a potential target for the criminal element to take your bag full of gear. ***The problem is that you cannot assume that others will leave you alone during a crisis especially if they believe you have something that will be of value to them.*** Never assume how someone may or may not react to you because you just do not know.

Military Style Bag

Many people advocate against using any type of military or tactical bag as it may cause you to stand out and become a target. I take a different approach on this topic. As I have said regarding the non-

Realistic Bug Out Bag

descript bag you cannot assume that others will leave you alone during a crisis. The alternative to this may be to purposefully carry a military/tactical looking bag to present an image that you are a **hard target** and that the criminal element should look elsewhere for a potential victim.

Maxpedition Condor II

Now in reality the type of bag you decide to carry is but one factor that a criminal will use to decide if you are a good target. "How" you carry yourself is a big determination to a criminal who needs to make a conscious decision to steal your gear. It is important to stand tall, look confident, and portray an image that you have the knowledge, skills, and abilities to protect yourself if necessary. If someone looks like they are targeting you be sure to look right into their eyes and acknowledge that you know what they are up to. Present a look that makes them want to choose someone else. If necessary, tell the potential criminal that you will rip their damn head off if they attempt anything. Maybe even throw in a few choice words to let them know you are serious. Even if you are just bluffing this tactic may work. But, it may not work so it is a good idea to be able to defend yourself just in case. The reality is that you may be out skilled, out gunned, or out numbered. In this case it may be better to give your pack and live to fight another day. It is a decision that you have to make.

Regardless of what kit you decide to build you need to make sure it is with you when an emergency occurs. This is a point that is often overlooked. Too many people incorrectly assume that they will be at home when a bug out situation occurs. Therefore they leave their kit at home. Disasters can occur at any time and you may find that you are not home. You might be at work, a sporting event, out to dinner, seeing a movie, at the park with your children, on vacation, etc. If you do not have your bug out bag with you the reality is that you may not have the time or ability to get home to get your bag. Yet, having your bag with you at all times can be problematic.

Being prepared to bug out is not always as easy as one would like. There are a lot of situations that can make carrying a bug out bag rather difficult and inconvenient. For example:

- What if you take public transportation (bus, train) to work?

- Do you carry your bug out bag with you on the bus, train, or light rail?

- Do you have a place at work to safely store your bag?

- Won't you stick out with your bag?

- If you are on vacation do you take a bug out bag with you?

- Is your bug out bag safe from theft if stored in your vehicle?

- If in your vehicle will hot temperature, cold temperature, or high humidity impact the contents of your kit?

- Do you work in a secure facility that does not allow weapons?

- If you carry your bug out bag with you will it cause you to stick out instead of blending in with your environment?

- Will your spouse or children have access to their bug out bags if they are not home?

- Do you have duplicate packs so one bug out bag is always at home and another is with you at work or in your vehicle?

- Is it possible to securely cache or store an extra bug out bag close to work?

- Is it realistic to have your bug out bag with you all of the time?

- Should you carry an "everyday carry" EDC bag with you daily instead of a bug out bag?

There are not necessarily easy or convenient answers to these questions. Additionally, your individual situation may pose other challenges. Only you can choose how, when, and where to carry and store your bug out bag. Personally, I do not feel it is realistic to carry my bug out bag everywhere I go. Instead, I carry an everyday carry (EDC) bag with me that has essential items. With my EDC bag I still have a lot of the same items as my bug out bag minus the amount of food, water, clothing, and shelter items. In some respect is can be considers a "lite bug out bag" that is more tuned to easily get me through the first 24 hours. It is very "low key" and does not draw attention to me yet it provides a lot of capability. I also have items stored in my vehicle that can add to and complement my EDC bag. Taken together these provide me with a lot of utility in an emergency. I also keep a small stash of items at work. No situation will be perfect and sometimes you have to make do with what you have. This is why it is important to be flexible and adaptable to whatever comes your way.

It is important to have a contingency plan for the time when all of your plans fail for whatever reason and you do not have access to your bug out bag or your everyday carry bag. In this situation you have to rely only on what you carry on your person. In terms of a bug out situation this can be considered the worst case scenario. But, all is not lost as you should always carry certain items on your person.

Following are items that you should always carry in addition to your wallet, keys, and cell phone:

- Pocket knife such as a Swiss Army Knife or a small multi-tool such as a Leatherman Juice

- Small Firesteel

- Lighter

- Small Flashlight that takes 1 AA lithium battery

- Small pill container attached to your keys to hold medicine or an over the counter pain reliever

- Paracord bracelet or necklace for rope which has multiple uses

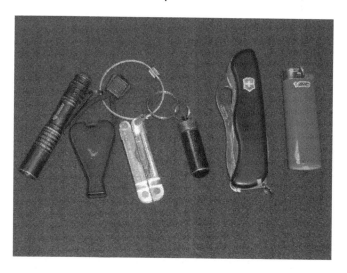

Streamlight MicroStream flashlight, JetScream whistle, Leatherman Micra (Juice is also a good option), pill container, Victorinox One Handed Trekker, and Bic lighter.

Optional items to consider carrying:

- JetScream whistle

- Emergency signaling mirror (place in wallet)

These items do not take up much room and provide an extreme amount of utility for their small size. Without these basic items you may find yourself in a bind without the ability to cut using a knife or start a fire with a lighter or rod. Never be caught without these items.

Depending on where you work or visit you may be prohibited from carrying a knife or any other weapon. In such a situation it is up to you to follow the rules or not. I don't mention a firearm in any of the above lists. If you can legally carry a firearm it would be prudent to do so. Unfortunately, we live in a society that is becoming more "firearm-phobic" and increasingly placing restrictions on your second amendment rights. I am a firm believer in the second amendment and the right of law abiding citizens the right to carry to protect themselves or loved ones. A firearm is a great equalizer for the weak to use against the strong.

Max Cooper

Bug Out Bag Assessment

This short assessment is designed to help you focus on the content and reasoning behind your bug out bag.

1. Are you *mentally* prepared to bug out?

    _____Yes

    _____No

2. Are you confident in your knowledge, skills, and abilities to bug out?

    _____Yes

    _____No

3. What length of time is your bug out bag designed to supply you for?

    _____1-3 days

    _____4-7 days

    _____8+ days

4. Do you know and understand the difference between "wants" and "needs" pertaining to the content of your kit?

   _____Yes

   _____No

5. To what location do you plan on bugging out? (This will help determine resources that are available to you and items you may need to carry with you.)

   _____

   _____

6. What level of physical conditioning are you?

   _____Couch Potato

   _____Average

   _____Peak Condition

7. What is the furthest you have ever walked with a backpack?

   _____1-5 miles

   _____6-10 miles

   _____11-15 mile

   _____16-20 miles

   _____21+ miles

8. Who will you be bugging out with?

   _____Myself

   _____Family

   _____Friends

   _____Prepper Network

9. Will you have children under the age of 15 or anyone over the age of 65 with you?

   _____Yes

   _____No

Realistic Bug Out Bag

10. Do you smoke?

    _____Yes
    _____No

11. Do you drink more than 4 alcoholic beverages per week?

    _____Yes
    _____No

12. Do you drink more than 2 caffeinated beverages per day?

    _____Yes
    _____No

13. Do you have any existing *medical* conditions that can impair your ability to effectively bug out?

    _____Yes
    _____No

14. Do you have any *psychological* conditions that can impair your ability to effectively bug out?

   _____Yes
   _____No

15. Do you take prescription medication on a daily basis?

   _____Yes
   _____No

16. Do you abuse prescription medication or use medications in a manner that differ from the directions in which they were prescribed?

   _____Yes
   _____No

17. Do you wear prescription eye glasses or contact lenses?

   _____Yes
   _____No

18. Can you <u>run</u> 1 mile in 10 minutes or less?

   _____Yes
   _____No

19. Do you eat at least two healthy meals per day?

   _____Yes
   _____No

20. Do you sleep at least 7 hours per night?

   _____Yes
   _____No

21. Do you use goal setting as a way to plan accomplishing your bug out goals?

   _____Yes
   _____No

Once you have completed this assessment go back and review your answers.

Based upon your answers:

1. Do you have the proper mindset, knowledge, and understanding of mental and physical skills to successfully bug out?

2. Are your lifestyle choices relating to sleep, exercise, and use of alcohol, tobacco, caffeine or prescription medication preventing you from performing at an effective level to bug out?

3. Do you have **clearly defined written goals** relating to fitness, lifestyle or skills along with a clear action plan to accomplish your bug out goals?

Once you have identified problematic answers develop an action plan and, if necessary, training regimen to improve deficient areas. The reality is that you cannot perform at a peak level in a crisis, especially a life or death crisis, without proper:

- Mindset
- Mental skills
- Physical skills
- Healthy lifestyle that includes a healthy diet, exercise, and stress management skills

Realistic Bug Out Bag

You owe it to yourself, family, friends, and those who love you to have the knowledge, skills, and ability to function at a peak performance during a crisis. The goal is not just to go home at the end of a bug out crisis but to go home healthy and unharmed. And then, you may have to rebuild your life depending on the impact of the incident.

Before proceeding any further I urge you to make a commitment to yourself that you will commit to developing an action plan and goals to improve any deficient areas that you have identified. Failure is not an option.

> **Will you commit right now to correcting any noted deficiencies?**
>
> _____Yes
>
> _____No

If you answered "***yes***" you have a chance at surviving.

If you answered "***no***" you fail to have the proper mindset and commitment to survival. You can stop reading at this point. This may sound harsh but knowledge without commitment and action is valueless. Only you can commit to taking positive steps to increase your chances at surviving a bug out situation.

Knowledge + Skills + Abilities + Commitment =

Increased chance of survival.

Even then, there are no guarantees.

Are you prepared?

Realistic Bug Out Bag

Kit Categories

Following are categories that are essential regardless of the purpose of your kit. There are a lot of people who put out acronyms for their requirements. I am not trying to come up with a fancy list, just a realistic list. The goal is to keep you alive. Also, some items can fit into more than one category because they have multiple uses.

Category	Potential Item
Cutting Tool	Fixed Blade Knife, Multi-tool, Pocket Knife
Fire	Ferrocerium Rod, Lighter, Matches, Cotton Balls with Vaseline
Water	Water 100 oz. minimum, 32 oz. Stainless steel water bottle, 32 oz. Nalgene bottle
Food	Meals and snacks, Esbit stove, Stainless Steel Pot
Shelter	Tarp, Emergency Blanket, Bivy, Rope, Duct Tape
Light	Headlamp, Flashlight, Batteries
Communication	AM/FM Radio, FRS/GMRS Radio, Ham Radio, Cell Phone, Extra Batteries
Clothing	Base Layers, Boots, Sunglasses, Gloves, Hat, Eye Protection
Medical	First Aid Kit, Prescription Glasses, Prescription Medication
Weapon	Handgun and Ammunition, Pepper Spray
Miscellaneous	Varies depending on your individualized and environmental circumstances

Do not confuse the contents of your bug out bag with a wilderness survival kit. While there may be some overlap these two kits are distinctively different and are designed for different purposes. For example, in a 72 hour kit you should not necessarily need snares, traps, or a fishing kit. If you live in an area where fishing is abundant you might decide to carry a fishing kit but this would not normally be part of a 72 hour bug out bag. Remember, you are in a constant struggle to keep your pack focused and light.

> ***Your goal is to have a bug out bag that is <u>light</u>, <u>mobile</u>, and <u>efficient</u>.***

Quality of Items

This is the area seems to warrant some very solid discussion and concern. More often than not people are looking for "less expensive" (read that as cheap) ways to obtain gear and items. **I strongly disagree with the concept of buying cheap gear.** I have done it in the past and it <u>NEVER</u> works out well. The outcome is <u>ALWAYS</u> bad. And in the long run you end up spending the money for quality gear to replace the cheap ineffective gear. Now believe me, I understand that money is tight for many people. I get it. In my experience I have always ended up replacing cheap gear with quality gear because the cheap gear does not work, fails to last, or does not perform as designed. When my butt is on the line this is unacceptable. If money is tight I recommend buying high quality gear at a slower pace and getting what you need. This will require prioritizing what you need vs. what you want. There is not much worse than having a bag full of useless gear that will not perform when needed the most and not finding out until you use it. When it comes to gear get the best quality that you can afford. If it comes down to having nothing for the time being then save your money until you can get what you need so that you cannot only depend on the gear but have confidence in its ability.

When putting together your bug out bag I highly recommend buying the best quality components that you can afford. Keep in mind that this kit is your "survival" kit for dealing with a less than ideal situation. Do not skimp on quality or you will pay the price when things go bad and your gear fails. Each item in your kits serves a purpose and is going to be a "need" not a want. This means that you are going to depend on each item in your kit to perform. Less expensive items are cheap for a reason. They cannot be depended on when needed the most. Do not put yourself in this situation. You will regret it if you do.

Max Cooper

Redundancy

The concept of redundancy is very important when discussing survival preparedness. It is important to carry backup of important items. For example, when it comes to flashlights I strongly believe in the concept of redundancy meaning that I carry an extra flashlight in case the flashlight fails, batteries die, or it gets knocked out of my hand. I highly recommend that you carry no less than two flashlights. You may hear people say the following phrase, "*Two is one; one is none*" which speaks directly to the concept of redundancy. Failures happen and batteries die – often at the worst possible time. Always have a back-up and embrace the concepts of redundancy! Remember, your unwelcome partner, Mr. Murphy, is ready to cause problems for you so anticipate problems and be ready with solutions to his devious methods. Redundancy helps to keep Murphy away!

Let's now examine each of the individual categories above and look at this in more detail. Keep in mind that you will need to adjust your bug out bag to your individualized needs. Therefore, I may list items that you would not consider or I may leave out items that you feel are absolutely required. Again, take away ideas that work for you and implement what you feel is needed for your particular situation. There are a lot of different ways to go with a bug out bag. Make your kit uniquely your own.

Realistic Bug Out Bag

Cutting Tool

Having a quality cutting tool is going to be one of your most valuable assets. Always try to have a knife on you at all times. The three items to consider are a fixed blade knife, multi-tool, and a pocket knife.

Fixed Blade Knife

When it comes to your knife I recommend a fixed blade full tang knife with a minimum blade length of 5 inches. A high quality knife is going to be one of the more expensive and heavy items in your kit. You may also want to get a knife that has a thick blade in case you need to use it to pry. Generally, you want to avoid using your knife as a pry bar but you might find yourself in a situation that requires such action. I recommend staying away from serrated blades and stick to a plain edge.

Options include:

- Ka-Bar Becker BK2 Campanion (Upgrade to Micarta handles)
- ESEE-5 Plain Blade
- ESEE-6 Plain Blade
- Ontario RAT-5

When it comes to fixed blade knives you have a ton of choices. I am a big fan of ESEE knives due to the quality of both the knife and the sheath. They also come with a great warranty. But, they are very expensive. Ka-Bar and Ontario are also good less expensive choices although I find that they sheaths tends to not be the best quality. Look for a fixed blade that fits your needs.

Your knife can also serve as a weapon for self-defense situations. Be aware that using a knife for self-defense is an up close and personal situation that is violent, brutal, and oftentimes very bloody. You would probably benefit from taking some training in knife fighting as it is not like you see in the movies. Consider knife-fighting a last resort as it requires that you get close to an adversary who also has the ability to harm you.

Becker BK-2 on top, Ontario RAT-5 on bottom.

Multi-Tool

As the name implies a multi-tool has multiple uses and is very versatile. I have owned and used a Leatherman Wave for years and it has been a great multi-tool for any purpose that I have needed it for. Multi-tools, as the name implies, comes with a lot of different tools such as: Pliers, wire cutter, knife, saw, can opener, screwdriver, scissors, file bottle opener, etc. that can come in handy during a bug out event. They come in a lot of sizes from small to large and from inexpensive to very expensive. If you take the time to conduct a little research you will find one that fits your needs.

Options include:

- Leatherman Wave
- Leatherman OHT Coyote Tan
- Gerber Black Diesel Multi-Plier
- SOG Specialty Knives & Tools PowerLock EOD 2.0 Scissor Multi-Tool

Again, you have a lot of choices with multi-tools. I recommend that you get one with pliers, non-serrated blade, saw, file, screw driver, Philips screwdriver, and scissors.

Leatherman Wave

Pocket Knife

When it comes to a pocket knife there are literally hundreds of great options available along a very large range of prices. The first question to consider is whether you want this knife to double as a "tactical fighting" knife. If so, this will steer you toward a specific type of knife. You can also go with a Swiss Army type of knife that can perform multiple functions but remember you should also have a multi-tool because it is larger, easier to manipulate, and provides more utility than a knife. There is no wrong answer to the question of what knife you should obtain. Whatever knife you choose needs to fit your needs.

Realistic Bug Out Bag

I recommend the following when choosing a pocket knife:

- Get one that has a locking blade
- Avoid a serrated blade as a straight blade is very effective without the added difficulty of sharpening
- Get a knife that allows you to deploy the blade one handed which is valuable if you are injured

When it comes to pocket knife recommendations there is a shear abundance of options that are available. If you stick with a name brand it is very hard to go wrong. Keep in mind that everyone has opinions when it comes to knives. Find one that fits your needs and not the needs or likes of another person. Like firearms, it is hard to get people to agree on knives.

Options to consider for an urban environment:

- Victorinox Swiss Army One Hand Trekker NS Pocket Knife
- Victorinox Swiss Army Knife Rescue Tool
- Victorinox Swiss Army Hunter XT Knife

Max Cooper

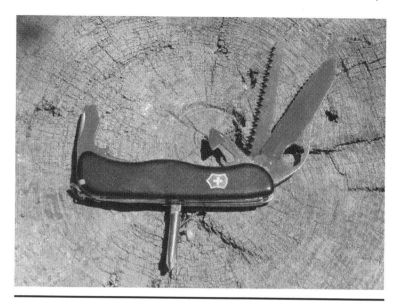

Victorinox One Handed Trekker

Wire Snips

In an urban environment wire snips can be a very valuable asset to allow you the ability to cut through fences in a relatively rapid manner. This can be especially important if you have members of your group who do not have the ability to climb over a fence. Also, the fence may have concertina or barbed wire making climbing over the fence not an option. Wire cutters are generally not expensive although they can be a little bigger than I would like. As with many items in your bag there is a cost/benefit ratio and you must decide if the item is worth having. Many multi-tools come with wire cutters but they may not be heavy duty enough and not have the ability to cut through fencing.

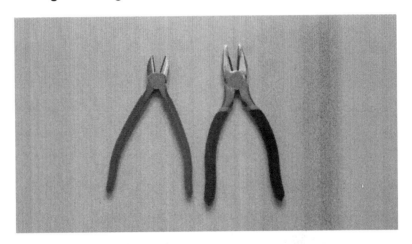

Hack Saw

Again, carrying a hack saw is generally geared toward an urban environment and can provide a fairly effective cutting tool. You can carry the blade only or you can carry a hack saw that has a small handle. If you decide to only carry the blade it is important to realize that you may not have the grip or leverage to be as effective as using one with a handle. Stanley makes some very inexpensive hack saws. If you decide to carry one I highly recommend putting some duct tape over the blade so that you do not accidently destroy anything in your pack.

In regard to wire snips and a hack saw it is clear that bolt cutters would be a more effective tool to cut through wire and locks. But, bolt cutters are not necessarily more efficient due to the larger size and increased weight. Also, they tend to be much more expensive. Always go back to the weight of an item to determine if you really want to add it to your bug out bag. Bolt cutters are a great tool but I'm not sure that I want to carry the extra weight over a long distance.

Realistic Bug Out Bag

Fire

Never take fire for granted and never resort to primitive fire starting methods. Survival is about conservation of calories, proper hydration, and body temperature regulation. If you have to use a primitive method to start a fire you have failed to properly prepare. Additionally, primitive fire starting is very difficult, tiring, burns a lot of calories, and does not guarantee fire. It can also cause serious blisters on your hands. You can expend a lot of energy using a primitive fire starting method and never get a fire started. In a bug out situation this is a very demoralizing feeling.

Benefits of fire include:

- The ability to cook food
- Warm up to prevent hypothermia
- Dry clothes that are wet
- Disinfect water
- Provides a light source
- Provides comfort and relaxation
- Use for signaling
- Can be used as a weapon
- Create a diversion

Fire serves many purposes and is one of the ultimate multi-purpose tools. But, it is also important to be careful with fire as you do not want to get burned or accidently start a fire beyond the size of your original intentions. Burns are very painful and can easily become infected so be very careful not to become injured. Take your time and respect fire. Never use fire in a confined space that lacks adequate ventilation.

There are plenty of methods available to start a fire that, with little training, almost always guarantees a fire.

Options include:

- Ferrocerium Rod
- Lighter
- Stormproof Matches

There is absolutely no reason not to carry all three of the above mentioned fire starting methods. They are small, compact, lightweight, and inexpensive. When used in conjunction with cotton balls mixed with Vaseline as your tinder you are guaranteed fire. Another option that you can use is alcohol preps. They are small, compact, very lightweight, and can be stored a long time as long as it is not stored in a hot environment like a vehicle. There are a lot of different items that you can use as tinder to help get your fire started. Most are small, compact and well worth having to get your fire going fast.

I highly recommend that you carry at least one ferrocerium rod and one lighter on your person and another set in your pack. Redundancy is important when it comes to fire. When you are cold and tired you want the ability to get a fire going very quickly with little effort. It becomes exponentially more difficult to start a fire if you are hypothermic or injured.

Fire Kit Version 1 (Soap Container): Bic lighter, cotton with Vaseline, WetFire tinder, UCO Stormproof matches, Light My Fire Firesteel, and mini light.

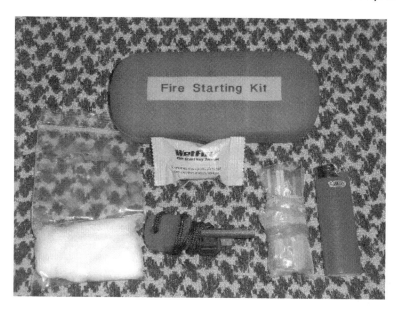

Fire Kit Version 2 (Eye Glass Case): Cotton with Vaseline, WetFire tinder, Light My Fire Firesteel, UCO Stormproof matches, and Bic Lighter.

Realistic Bug Out Bag

Exotac Matchcap – Capable of holding long UCO and REI Stormproof matches.

Max Cooper

Water

Simply put: **Water is life.** One of the heaviest items you will carry is water. And, it is one of the most important. If you live in a warm climate water is absolutely essential especially if you have to bug out on foot. But, water is still critical in a cold environment where people do not drink enough because of the cold temperature. Regardless of where you are located you need water. At a minimum, I recommend a backpack that holds a 100 ounce water hydration bladder. On top of that I recommend that you carry a 32 ounce stainless steel water bottle and a 32 ounce Nalgene bottle. This will provide you with 164 ounces of water which seems like a lot but it is not. Weight wise 164 ounces weighs about 10.7 pounds which is significant. If weight is becoming an issue do not waste your water, drink it or cook with it. Do not necessarily drink all at once but try to consume about 16 ounces each hour. If you drink too much too soon you may get sick and vomit which is never good during a survival situation.

Try never to go below 50 ounces of water. Also, if you do not know if drinkable water sources are going to be available then top off your water at every opportunity. If you are absolutely sure that you will have a drinkable form of water available then the minimum amount of recommended water to carry is the 100 ounces of water in your water bladder. People often refer to weight as either good weight or bad weight. While water is heavy it is definitely good weight as you must have water to survive. If you do not have access to a water source then carry 164 ounces. For a three day bug out I try to dedicate at least 24 ounces of water for cooking dehydrated meals which require boiled water.

My go to hydration bladder is the Geigerrig 3 liter, 100 oz. Hydration Engine which costs about $45.00. It is very strong, easy to clean, and uses a pump system so that you do not have to suck the water from the tube as it squirts into your mouth. This might not seem like a big deal but when you are hot and fatigued it really makes a difference. Also, because the water tube is pressurized you can share your water with another person without them having to place their mouth on your tube. You can also squirt the water to irrigate a wound or on your head to cool off. No other hydration system works using a pressurized bladder. Geigerrig is a very nice system.

If water is going to be a concern such as in dry climates, desert environments, during a heat wave, or water sources become contaminated you can carry collapsible water containers. A great container is the Platypus PlusBottle which can hold 1 liter of water, is lightweight, durable, and collapsible when empty. It also has an attachment that you can attach it to your gear if necessary. This is also a great backup system should your hydration bladder have a catastrophic failure and is no longer capable of holding water. Remember, Mr. Murphy is ready to mess with you at every opportunity. Being properly prepared will help keep him at bay.

Along with having plenty of water consider carrying some electrolyte replacement powder packets especially in a hot climate. When you sweat a lot you are losing valuable electrolytes from your body. There are a lot of powdered electrolyte brands to choose from, they come in small individualized packets, come in a variety of flavors, are inexpensive, and can mask the taste of water that has been filtered from a non-traditional water source. If you have children who do not like to drink water and are concerned that they are not drinking enough, put flavored electrolyte powder in their water and they will be more apt to drink which will help keep them hydrated.

A lot of people talk about carrying an unlubricated condom to carry water. I do **not** recommend this as condoms are too delicate, can easily break, and because you can purchase a product like the Platypus which, while bulkier, is much more durable and effective. It is also difficult to carry a condom full of water and maintain situational awareness of potential threats in your environment while walking in an area with a lot of potential unknown factors. Some will say that you can put the condom full of water inside a sock for added durability. If that is what you want to do then go for it. I'm not wasting my energy on this endeavor and neither should you.

If you are unsure if the water is drinkable do not drink the water. This is especially important for children, the elderly, or those with compromised immune systems. Even if you are very healthy you will need to utilize methods to disinfect the water. This can include boiling, iodine, water filter or water purification tablets such as Katadyn Micropur Water Purification Tablets. You can use your 32 ounce stainless steel water bottle to boil water if necessary.

Common waterborne diseases include:

Cryptosporidium[ii]

Cryptosporidium is a microscopic parasite that causes the diarrheal disease cryptosporidiosis. Both the parasite and the disease are commonly known as "Crypto."

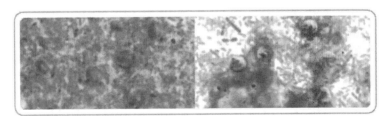

There are many species of Cryptosporidium that infect humans and animals. The parasite is protected by an outer shell that allows it to survive outside the body for long periods of time and makes it very tolerant to chlorine disinfection.

While this parasite can be spread in several different ways, water (drinking water and recreational water) is the most common method of transmission. Cryptosporidium is one of the most frequent causes of waterborne disease among humans in the United States.

Cryptosporidium Treatment[iii]

Most people who have healthy immune systems will recover without treatment. Diarrhea can be managed by drinking plenty of fluids to prevent dehydration. People who are in poor health or who have weakened immune systems are at higher risk for more severe and prolonged illness. Young children and pregnant women may be more susceptible to dehydration resulting from diarrhea and should drink plenty of fluids while ill. Rapid loss of fluids from diarrhea may be especially life threatening to babies. Therefore, parents should talk to their health care providers about fluid replacement therapy options for infants.

Anti-diarrheal medicine may help slow down diarrhea, but a health care provider should be consulted before such medicine is taken.

Nitazoxanide has been FDA-approved for treatment of diarrhea caused by Cryptosporidium in people with healthy immune systems and is available by prescription. However, the effectiveness of nitazoxanide in immunosuppressed individuals is unclear.

Giardia[iv]

Giardia is a microscopic parasite that causes the diarrheal illness known as giardiasis. Giardia (also known as Giardia intestinalis, Giardia lamblia, or Giardia duodenalis) is found on surfaces or in soil, food, or water that has been contaminated with feces (poop) from infected humans or animals.

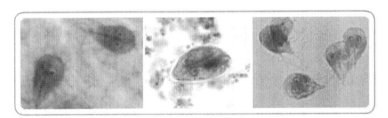

Giardia is protected by an outer shell that allows it to survive outside the body for long periods of time and makes it tolerant to chlorine disinfection. While the parasite can be spread in different ways, water (drinking water and recreational water) is the most common method of transmission.

Giardia Treatment[v]

Several drugs can be used to treat Giardia infection. Effective treatments include metronidazole, tinidazole, and nitazoxanide. Alternatives to these medications include paromomycin, quinacrine, and furazolidone. Some of these drugs may not be routinely available in the United States.

Different factors may shape how effective a drug regimen will be, including medical history, nutritional status, and condition of the immune system. Therefore, it is important to discuss treatment options with a health care provider.

Leptospirosis[vi]

Leptospirosis is a bacterial disease that affects humans and animals. It is caused by bacteria of the genus Leptospira. In humans, it can cause a wide range of symptoms, some of which may be mistaken for other diseases. Some infected persons, however, may have no symptoms at all.

Without treatment, Leptospirosis can lead to kidney damage, meningitis (inflammation of the membrane around the brain and spinal cord), liver failure, respiratory distress, and even death.

Leptospirosis Treatment[vii]

Leptospirosis is treated with antibiotics, such as doxycycline or penicillin, which should be given early in the course of the disease. Intravenous antibiotics may be required for persons with more severe symptoms.

There are many other bacterial, viral, and protozoa diseases that can be obtained from consuming contaminated water.

Water Treatment Methods[viii]:

> ***Except for boiling, few of the water treatment methods are 100% effective in removing all pathogens.***

Boiling:

Boiling can be used as a pathogen reduction method that should kill all pathogens. Water should be brought to a rolling boil for 1 minute. At altitudes greater than 6,562 feet, you should boil water for 3 minutes.

Filtration:

Filtration can be used as a pathogen reduction method against most microorganisms, depending on the pore size of the filter, amount of the contaminant, particle size of the contaminant, and charge of the contaminant particle. Manufacturer's instructions must be followed. Only filters that contain a chemical disinfectant matrix will be effective against some viruses.

Disinfection:

Disinfection can be used as a pathogen reduction method against microorganisms. However, contact time, disinfectant concentration, water temperature, water turbidity (cloudiness), water pH, and many other factors can impact the effectiveness of chemical disinfection. The length of time and concentration of disinfectant varies by manufacturer and effectiveness of pathogen reduction depends on the product. Depending on these factors, 100% effectiveness may not be achieved. Manufacturer's instructions must be followed.

If boiling water is not possible, a combination of filtration and chemical disinfection is the most effective pathogen reduction method.

Other treatment methods can be effective against some of the above pathogens:

Ultraviolet Light (UV Light):

Ultraviolet Light can be used as a pathogen reduction method against some microorganisms. The technology requires effective prefiltering due to its dependence on low water turbidity (cloudiness), the correct power delivery, and correct contact times to achieve maximum pathogen reduction. UV might be an effective method in pathogen reduction in backcountry water; there is a lack of independent testing data available on specific systems. Manufacturer's instructions must be followed.

MIOX®:

MIOX® systems use a salt solution to create mixed oxidants, primarily chlorine. Chlorine has a low to moderate effectiveness in killing Giardia, and a high effectiveness in killing bacteria and viruses. Manufacturer's instructions must be followed.

Important:

Water that has been disinfected with iodine is NOT recommended for pregnant women, people with thyroid problems, those with known hypersensitivity to iodine, or continuous use for more than a few weeks at a time.

Emergency Disinfection of Drinking Water[ix]

If a community or well water system with clean water is not available, it is important to find safe water or disinfect water for drinking, cooking, and brushing teeth.

U.S. federal agencies and the Red Cross recommend these same four steps to disinfect drinking water in an emergency.

1. Use bottled water that has not been exposed to flood waters if it is available.

2. If you don't have bottled water, you should boil water to make it safe. Boiling water will kill most types of disease-causing organisms that may be present. If the water is cloudy, filter it through clean cloths or allow it to settle, and draw off the clear water for boiling. Boil the water for one minute, let it cool, and store it in clean containers with covers.

3. If you can't boil water, you can disinfect it using household bleach. Bleach will kill some, but not all, types of disease-causing organisms that may be in the water (Chlorine and iodine may not be effective in controlling more resistant organisms like Cryptosporidium). If the water is cloudy, filter it through clean cloths or allow it to settle, and draw off the clear water for disinfection. Add 1/8 teaspoon (or 8 drops) of regular, unscented, liquid household bleach for each gallon of water, stir it well, and let it stand for 30 minutes before you use it. Store disinfected water in clean containers with covers.

4. If you have a well that has been flooded, the water should be tested and disinfected after flood waters recede. If you suspect that your well may be contaminated, contact your local or state health department for specific advice.

Food

Most people do not add food to their bug out bag stating that they can survive three days without food. Technically this is true; practically it is foolish. My question to you is: *Have you ever gone three days without food?* If not, do you want to do it during a crisis where your body is stressed and you may have to be on your feet for hours at a time while burning a lot of calories. This isn't about bravado or thumping your chest. Yes, you can survive three days without food but you will be grumpy, tired, and not thinking or performing at your best. Your body needs fuel to run effectively. Food will not only make you feel better but eating a meal will force you to slow down and rest which many people forget to do during a crisis.

When it comes to food there are many choices such as trail mix, beef jerky, sealed pouches of tuna or salmon, nuts, energy bars, packets of raw honey, and dehydrated meals. Dehydrated meals are tasty and provide a lot of calories in a relatively small package. The days of horrid tasting dehydrated meals are long gone. I prefer Mountain House meals as they taste great and are easy to prepare. The one drawback is that they require water so you must dedicate some of your water supply to cooking. If you do not have water you can't use these meals. The extra weight of the water will be used during the cooking process and again it will force you to stop and eat. When you eat you will also drink water. This will allow you to use water wisely, lower your pack weight, and stay hydrated. This is a win-win situation.

It is important to remember that during a crisis you will be amped up from the stress hormones that are released into your blood stream. Many people simply forget to eat as they are focused on the situation and not eating. Even if you are not hungry your body is still burning calories that need to be replaced so at a minimum snack on a protein bar, nuts, or a bag of tuna fish. Your body will appreciate the nourishment from these needed calories.

Do not fall into the trap that you do not need food in your bug out bag. You do! Not having food to eat will make your bug out more difficult and challenging. And when you get hungry you will start thinking about food when you might benefit from thinking about other required tasks. Having the ability to survive for up to 30 days without food does not mean I want to purposefully put myself in such a situation. Even for 3 days I am going to want to eat food for the nourishment that it will provide. Additionally, I have tested myself and gone 3 full days without any food. It has taught me that I am going to definitely include food in my bug out bag. If you choose differently you are making a big mistake.

Since I am only referring to a 72 hour bug out I am not going to take a significant cooking system. I am going to go low tech and use an Esbit Stove with fuel tabs to warm water in a titanium cup for my dehydrated meals. The reason for this is because the Esbit stove is basic, compact, easy to use, and will not break down. It also eliminates the need to carry fuel for fuel stoves such as the MSR Pocket Rocket. My goal is to only cook three dehydrated meals during the 72 hours. That is only 1 meal per day. The rest of my food is going to be beef jerky, nuts, protein bars, etc. Because of this I am not opting to carry a stove that requires fuel canisters. Again, depending on the situation and where you live you may need to use a stove such as the MSR Pocket Rocket due to high winds or other factors. The MSR Pocket Rocket is a small and reliable stove that works great for small meals. The drawback is that you need to carry enough fuel. If you are bugging out with other people you can spread the fuel among other group members if necessary.

For eating my dehydrated meal I use the Light My Fire Titanium Spork. At 17 grams or .60 ounces this will satisfy those who count ounces and keep weight to a minimum. It is also much more durable than a plastic spork. Titanium is very strong and durable although this spork is capable of being bent. Additionally, it will not corrode, rust, and it is hypoallergenic. It fits good in my hands and is easy to use for different types of food for the most part.

Esbit stove with Snow Peak titanium cup.

Mountain House meal with Light My Fire Titanium spork.

Realistic Bug Out Bag

Light My Fire Titanium Spork Basics:

Spoon: Very large and great for using with dehydrated meals such as Mountain House. Some people may find the spoon to be too big and uncomfortable. The spoon is probably too big for children to use and appears to be designed more for adults.

Fork: Good for using with softer foods. The tips of the fork are not as pointy as most forks used in dinnerware so it is a little more challenging when using with a well done steak or any meat that is tough. In a bug out situation I'm not going to be eating steak so this will not be an issue. Works well with Spaghetti and other types of noodles.

Knife: The knife is located on the side of the fork. For obvious reasons it is not very sharp. The serrations are not long and are dull so it will not cut your mouth but it is also not very functional for cutting food either. I'm not really convinced that there is much utility to the knife unless used on very soft food such as pancakes.

The real benefits of this spork is that it is extremely lightweight and durable for its size.

Max Cooper

Shelter

When referring to shelter it is often environmental factors that will dictate which form of shelter that you use. Because you may have to travel by foot you must consider a very minimalist lightweight shelter system. It will not provide the comforts of home and it is not designed to provide such comforts. When referring to shelter systems there are a lot of options to choose. Remember, your goal is to be light, mobile, and efficient.

Shelter options include:

- Tarp
- Emergency Blanket
- Bivvy Sack
- 55 Gallon Garbage Bag
- Hammock
- Tent

Tarp

For a tarp you can use a 5'x7' or 8'x10' tarp. Personally, I prefer to use an 8'x10' size tarp due to its larger size. Either one can provide shelter from the sun, rain, and snow and are capable of being configured in a host of ways. You can make a nice lean-to type shelter with an 8'x10' tarp that protects you from the ground and the sun. There are many types of tarps available ranging in price from very inexpensive to very expensive. A very expensive option is the Terra Nova Tarp Shelter 2 which is 8'x10' and weighs 11.7 ounces. You could also go with a standard 8'x10' tarp that you find in your local hardware store for around ten dollars. It should last for three days but they will not stand up to much abuse. The rivets tend to come loose and they can easily rip. Duct tape can be used to conduct repairs. There are a lot of tarps available in different price ranges so you should be able to find on that fits in your budget. Remember, you get what you pay for with your survival equipment. When using a tarp I highly recommend carrying 4-6 quality tent stakes.

Emergency Blanket

A good option for an emergency blanket is the Adventure Medical Kits SOL Emergency Blanket (1-Person) which weighs only 2.9 ounces, is small, and very versatile. The SOL Emergency Blanket is also available in a 2 person version which is bigger. These are so small, compact, and lightweight that you can carry 3-4 with you. Another option is the Grabber Outdoors Original Space Brand All Weather Blanket which comes with a hood and reflects up to 90% of your body heat. If you are in a very cold environment you may decide to go with a 100% wool blanket which is a great option although it is much larger and heavier. Italian wool blankets are very popular but have become difficult to find and have become very expensive if you do find one.

Bivvy

Adventure Medical Kits offers a few different bivy options.

- SOL Emergency Bivvy, 84" X 36" which is 8.5 oz. This bivy is small and lightweight.

- Sol Two Person Emergency Bivvy Blanket which is 84" X 60" and reflects up to 90% of radiated body heat.

- Thermolite 2.0 Bivvy which is more durable and reusable.

Bivvy options other than Adventure Medical Kits include:

- Blizzard Survival Sleeping Bag (Bivvy) - Tactical / Reversible

- US Military Surplus Bivy Sleeping Bag Cover Gore Tex

- Outdoor Research Helium Bivy (expensive option)

- MSR AC-Bivy (expensive option)

55 Gallon Garbage Bag

For the hardcore minimalist you might decide on a 55 gallon, 3 mil garbage bag. They are small, lightweight, and nothing fancy but it can serve a purpose in an emergency situation. These bags can provide shelter from the sun and rain and insulation from the cold ground when placed over an insulating material such as ground leaves.

Sleeping Bag and/or Sleeping Pad

Bringing along a sleeping bag and/or sleeping pad will generally be determined by your environment and climate conditions. Generally, these items do not weigh much and there are a lot of lightweight options available. The problem is that they can add bulk to your bug out bag. You can get a down sleeping bag that will compress to the size of a football or just a little bigger. If your environment dictates that you need a sleeping bag try to get one that is made of down and is rated for the lowest temperature that you will encounter. It is critical that you do not get a down sleeping bag wet or it will lose its insulation capability. If you are in a very cold climate it becomes more difficult to get a cold weather sleeping bag that will compress to a small size. Yet, you cannot afford to go without this item or you can literally freeze to death. A good sleeping pad will help keep you insulated from the cold ground. Sleeping pads are generally lightweight but can be bulky if you choose foam. Therm-A-Rest sleeping pads tend to be more compact and provide good insulation from the cold ground.

Hammock

Another potential option is a hammock. The benefit of a hammock is that it is small, lightweight, compressible, and easy to set up. I have also found them to be very comfortable to sleep in. If it is cold outside you may need to use an insulating layer on the bottom of the hammock to keep you warm. The other factor is that you need a place that is capable of attaching the hammock. In the woods this is very easy but in an urban environment this may pose a significant challenge.

A hammock is a good option for the woods but may be more challenging in an urban environment.

Realistic Bug Out Bag

Regardless of the emergency shelter system that you choose to carry it is imperative that you carry 50'-100' of paracord, duct tape (Gorilla Brand) wrapped around a gift card, and I highly recommend at least 4-6 quality tent stakes. Your shelter system may not be pretty or even comfortable but it can keep you alive and provide a layer of protection from the elements such as sun, wind, snow, dust, and rain.

Generally, I avoid using a tent for a 3 day bug out situation. But, weather conditions may dictate that a tent is necessary. Rain, snow, excessive wind, or even the need for privacy may require that you use a tent. In such situations, I recommend using the smallest and lightest tent possible. If you are traveling by yourself use a one person tent. If you have a family your options become more limited as the bigger the tent the more weight you will need to carry and the more room it will take up. If you are bugging out with your family try to spread the weight among family members. Keep in mind that you will be as fast as the slowest member of your family.

If you have young children or older adults with you then expect to move more slowly. This can become a very challenging situation if the need to move conflicts with the speed of the slowest member of your party. There are no easy answers to this situation. Personally, I will never leave a family member behind. I will not compromise the safety and security of my family. Neither should you.

Max Cooper

Light

Light is another area that is commonly neglected yet is very important. You may end up hunkering down in a building that has no electricity. If the power grid goes down you will wish you had a light to illuminate the dark. This is especially true if you have young children with you. Bad people tend to hide in the shadows and light is one method that you can use to prevent unexpected run ins. For young children light is the perfect defense against the boogeyman.

There are three types of light that you should consider:

1. Headlamp
2. Flashlight
3. Glow sticks

Headlamp

The benefit of a headlamp is that it allows your hands to remain free to conduct required tasks. Many headlamps come with different colored lenses which can be beneficial depending on your needs. A solid headlamp to consider is the Petzl Tactikka XP Headlamp which has interchangeable red, green, blue and transparent wide-angle lenses. At about $56.00 it is pricey but it is excellent quality and works great. There are many other quality headlamps to choose from all of which will perform well.

Flashlight

There are so many flashlight options available that I am not going to recommend a specific light. What I will recommend is that you avoid flashlights that take CR123 as they are expensive and can be difficult to obtain. With current flashlight technology you can get a very high quality flashlight that uses AA batteries. These lights will be bright enough for most of your needs. Also, do not get wrapped up in the number of lumens that the light has unless you are planning on using the light for tactical or self-defense situations. Too many people get wrapped up in numbers when it comes to output, such as Lumens, in flashlights. They will adamantly argue that they "need" 225 or higher output of Lumens as opposed to 125 Lumens. I have conducted numerous tests comparing different Lumens and most people either can't tell the difference in brightness or state there is only a slight difference in output. Yes, there is a significant difference between an 80 Lumen light vs. a 300 Lumen light but you still must ask if you truly need 300 plus Lumens in a light. Only you can answer that question.

Things to consider with a flashlight:

- LED bulbs are a must

- Get a light that will not roll if it falls to the ground. Many come with a bezel that will prevent rolling.

- Get a light that has multiple output (low, medium, high) options so that you are not stuck using one setting which will eat up your batters especially when a lower setting will work fine.

- Have a flashlight that has a lanyard

- Always have a minimum of two flashlights for redundancy

Batteries

Whenever you carry electronics you will need to carry spare batteries. I like Energizer Lithium batteries because they last a long time and they are very light. Unfortunately, they are much more expensive than alkaline batteries. When carrying spare batteries it is best to use a carrier. I am very partial to Storacell by PowerPax. They are very inexpensive yet high quality and they come in a variety of different colors if you want to use a color coded system. They keep all of your batteries together and organized well. Do not put batteries in a zip lock back or other container in a loose format. It is always best to use a battery container.

I highly recommend that all batteries in your bug out bag are replaced on an annual basis. The batteries will still be fine to use if they have been stored for just a year. But, this will insure that every battery in your kit is always good to go. Also, I recommend that you do not leave batteries in your electronics because they can corrode which will ruin the electronic device.

Glow Sticks

The benefit of glow sticks is that they are light, small, effective, and last a long time. I prefer the Cyalume SnapLight Industrial Grade Light Sticks which last for 12 hours and can be purchased in packs of 10. Additionally, a lot of different colors are available. You could potentially develop a system of using certain colors as a form of covert communications.

If you have children these glow sticks can be fun for them to use at night. You can also attach a glow stick to your children at night so that you can easily see them in the dark. You do not want to lose your children at night in a bug out situation.

Communications

Communication is often under-rated in importance. Yet, communication both one-way and two-way communications can provide you with relevant information that will assist in your decision making especially during a bug out situation. One form of communications that has been proven ineffective time and time again is cellular phone service which is not reliable during a natural disaster or man-made crisis. Still, the majority of people rely exclusively on their cell phone for emergency communications not realizing the limitations. This lack of reliability has multiple causes but there are two main reasons that will concern you.

1. The event that is causing you to bug out may destroy part of the network rendering cell phone calls impossible.

2. Even when the network is not damaged the amount of people using the system will very quickly overwhelm its capabilities rendering the system ineffective.

Realistic Bug Out Bag

Types of communication:

	One-Way Comms	Two-Way Comms
AM/FM/SW Radio	X	
FRS/GMRS Radio		X
Amateur Radio		X

AM/FM Radio

Everyone is familiar with AM/FM radio since they are such popular radios.

AM

- Ranges from 535 to 1705 kilohertz
- Poorer sound quality compared to FM
- Can be transmitted over long distances
- Smaller bandwidth so it can have more stations available in any frequency range
- Often used for talk rather than music, i.e. talk radio and news
- Susceptible to atmospheric and electrical interference

FM

- Ranges from 88 to 108 megahertz
- Less prone to interference than AM
- Has greater sound quality due to higher bandwidth
- Commonly used for music; not talk

One of the benefits of having a radio is that they are so readily available and come in all shapes, sizes, and price ranges. You can also obtain an emergency AM/FM radio that has shortwave radio and NOAA weather. Additionally, in the event of a crisis you can be sure that both AM and FM stations are going to be reporting important news and information updates on a regular basis.

Grundig Mini 300

Realistic Bug Out Bag

    Many AM/FM radios also come with shortwave (SW) which can offer you the ability to obtain information as well during a crisis. Generally, local information from an AM/FM station will be all that you need during your bug out.

Weather radios from Midland and Ambient Weather.

FRS/GMRS Radio

    It is common to find FRS/GMRS radios combined into one radio and then advertised as "Up to 36 Miles" for communications. If you read the small print it states that obtaining 36 miles is under optimal conditions that, for the most part, are unrealistic. I have yet to meet anyone who was even able to obtain 15 miles from such a radio. I have conducted numerous tests with different brand radios and 2 miles seems to be the best I am able to obtain in an urban environment.

Max Cooper

Pros:

- Generally inexpensive
- Readily available
- No license required for FRS
- Typically uses a common power source
- Because these radio are common and used often they can be a source of intelligence during a disaster or crisis

Cons:

- License is required for GMRS ($85 for 5 years, no test required)
- Limited range generally in the area of <2 miles
- Frequencies can be very crowded
- FRS is limited to .5 watts

FRS/GMRS radios are a good option when you want to have contact with your group members over a relatively short difference. Unfortunately, channels can get crowded with a lot of clutter which can be frustrating during a crisis. You can use "privacy codes" but realize that they offer no privacy at all and your communications can still be overheard by others. FRS channels provide .5 watts and GMRS provide up to 5 watts. GMRS radios require a license although in an emergency anyone is authorized by the FCC to operate on a GMRS frequency. In a bug out situation you may need a more robust FRS/GMRS radio due to weather conditions. An excellent option in this situation is the Midland GXT5000.

Midland GXT5000 Mil-Spec FRS/GMRS radio.

The Midland GXT5000 36-Mile 22-Channel FRS/GMRS Two-Way Radio is a nice radio IF you need one that is built to military specs; meets IP67 dust infiltration requirements; and is waterproof to 3.2 feet. If you do not need a radio to meet such specs you may want to consider going with the less expensive Midland GXT1000VP4 36-Mile 50-Channel FRS/GMRS Two-Way Radio which is sold in pairs. One thing worth noting up front is that the GXT5000 does not perform any better than any other FRS/GMRS radios. They all put out the same amount of watts. The "military specs" marketing applies to the radios case and has nothing to do with performance. Radio performance is based on a lot of different factors. Even then do not expect to get a range of anywhere near 36 miles.

The Midland GXT5000 comes with a lot of features and is very easy to use as long as you read the user manual. Switching functions is easy and quick. You have a lot of options to set up the radio that will best fit your needs.

Following are aspects that I like about the GXT5000:

- The display is green and easy to read
- It comes with a lithium ion battery that is 2200mAh
- It comes with two belt clip options
- The radio comes with a nice desktop charger
- Setting privacy codes is easy (Note: privacy codes do NOT provide you with privacy and your conversation is capable of being heard by others.)

- The radio has a keypad lock to prevent accidentally changing radio settings.
- There is a silent operation if you need to maintain noise discipline. This feature will allow you to silent all beeps and tones.
- There is a "Time Out Time" that can be set to 15, 30, 45, 60 seconds or completely turned off. This can limit the time that someone is allowed to transmit.
- There is an "Out-of-Range Alert" that will alert you if you and another radio are outside of transmitting range. Both radios have to be set the same for this feature to work.
- You have a "Dual Watch Function" to monitor 2 channels. But, you cannot use this feature if you are using the Out-of-Range Alert. You must choose one or the other but not both.

Aspects about this radio that I do not like:

- Sold in single units and not pairs as with most FRS/GMRS radios
- Expensive
- If you use an external speaker/microphone jack you lose the waterproof protection

The Midland GXT5000 36-Mile 22-Channel FRS/GMRS Two-Way Radio is a nice option if you need mil-spec requirements. You will not get any better performance out of the radios so if mil-spec is not needed I would recommend a less expensive FRS/GMRS radio that is sold in pairs. The GXT5000, while made in China, seems to be well made and I have not encountered any issues.

Amateur Radio

Amateur radio is a very large and diverse field with numerous levels of licenses. The current levels from the lowest to the highest are: Technician, General, and Extra. There are some older classifications still around such as Novice but these will be irrelevant if you are going for your license. Additionally, Morse code is NO longer required for your testing. If you want the most capability to communicate over a long distance you really must consider obtaining your Technician's license. It is a 35 question test and all of the test questions are available for free on the Internet. There are also online practice exams that you can take for free.[x] With a little time, motivation, and effort you can easily pass the test thereby dramatically increasing your communication ability.

	Watts	Channels	License Required	Cost of License	Term of License
Amateur Radio	1-5 Mobile	Thousands	Yes	$15 test	10 Years

Realistic Bug Out Bag

Regarding the distance you will get with any radio it is important to understand that there are a lot of variables that impact the effectiveness of ALL radios. Such variables include: Number of watts, antenna, weather conditions, location, obstructions, your knowledge of your equipment, etc.

The pinnacle of emergency two-way radio communications is clearly amateur radio. This form of communication, depending on your individualized needs, will provide you with the best range of two-way communications.

Pros:

- Significant distance with the use of repeaters and linked repeaters

- Can use an external antenna to increase range

- Available in handy talkie, vehicle mounted, or base station

- Literally thousands of frequency options

- Many radio options to choose from

- Wattage output varies from 5 watts with a handy talkie to over 1,500 watts for a base station

Cons:

- Requires a license
- More technical to use
- Depending on the radio you purchase it can be expensive

Recommendations:

There are many choices when it comes to amateur radio. Basically, you cannot go wrong if you purchase a Yaesu, Icom, or Kenwood radio. Each of these brands offer high quality radios. Personally, I prefer Yaesu radios. This in no way diminishes the quality of Icom or Kenwood. Baofeng radios are becoming very popular but I do not recommend these radios as they are known for quality control issues. In a bug out situation I need to be able to rely on my gear. One of the main reasons of the popularity of the Baofeng radio is based solely on their low price. You can obtain one of these radios for $30-$50. Remember, you get what you pay for. I recommend that you stick with a name brand radio.

Yaesu FT-60

The Yaesu FT-60R DualBand Handheld 5W VHF/UHF Amateur Radio Transceiver - Dual Band is an excellent entry level radio especially for new ham radio operators.

Realistic Bug Out Bag

Yaesu FT-60 with external mic.

Pros:

- 5 Watts of Power
- 1000 Memory Channels
- Dual band VHF/UHF for 2M and 70cm
- NOAA Weather Alerts
- User manual is well written
- High quality; durable product
- Decent battery life
- Sound clarity is very good

- Lots of accessories are available
- The radio has a lot of options and functions to change different settings to your preference
- Easy to program
- Easy to clone

Cons:

- A bit bulkier compared to newer radios
- If you are not using WIRES then turn it off otherwise you will have a delay when transmitting

Yaesu FT-60 Recommendations:

1. Upgrade the antenna to the Diamond SRH77CA

2. Get the Vertex Standard Alkaline Battery Case (FBA-25) which will allow you to use 6 AA alkaline batteries for power should your NiMH battery lose power. Yaesu does not recommend using rechargeable batteries.

Cell Phone

Earlier I stated that cell phones are notoriously unreliable in a crisis. But, you should still carry one on you because it may work and it is small. Additionally, if the network is up and running you have access to a lot of information especially if you own a smartphone that provides you access to the internet, email, and apps.

Batteries

Batteries for an AM/FM radio should be able to last three days of constant use depending on the functionality of the radio. A cell phone and amateur radio on the other hand can go through batteries much faster especially during a crisis or emergency where you may be talking more than usual. In such situations it is important to have extra batteries or a battery backup power supply which is beneficial because they are often capable of charging many different types of batteries used in electronic equipment. Also, some amateur radios will also work in conjunction with AA batteries using a power pack designed to hold these size batteries.

Max Cooper

Clothing

I am not going to discuss all the variables that go into clothing. The key is to dress in layers that is appropriate for the environment that you live. When possible it is a good idea to wear quick drying clothes and clothes that offer SPF protection against the harmful UV rays of the sun. This will be especially important if you have to walk for miles.

In general, I do not advocate carrying a lot of extra clothing due to the bulk. Carry what you need for layers but not a lot extra. The exceptions to this are socks and underwear. Always carry an extra pair of each.

Items of special importance include:

Boots and Socks

Even if your bug out is only for three days you need to protect your feet. If your feet get injured you will lose your ability to remain mobile which can be a very dangerous situation that severely limits your bug out options. When getting boots there are a lot of choices and many brands are very durable and comfortable. Get boots that are waterproof and try to keep your feet dry. When it comes to socks I recommend two pair of 100% merino wool. It is also a wise idea to carry a small container of baby powder. If you have to walk for a long distance and the situation allows you should stop at least every two hours to rest your feet. Take off your boots, remove your socks and let your feet breathe for a little bit. Before putting your socks back on put some baby powder on your feet. If you feel a blister coming on or a hot spot you must immediately address this issue. Do NOT wait and try to tough it out or you will pay. Use some mole skin and take care of blisters and hot spots at the first sign. If you do not these situations will only get worse making an already bad situation much more difficult and challenging. Bottom line: Take care of your feet.

Hat

A wide brim boonie style hat is another must. You want to keep the sun off of your face and neck. Additionally, a wide brim hat will help to protect your eyes from the sun, rain, and snow. There are many styles of hats and some even offer SPF protection. The hat should have a lanyard to keep in on your head in windy conditions. Try to get a hat that will allow for use with a headlamp. The hat you choose, like all of your clothing, is strictly about utility and not fashion. It is to serve a purpose and not necessarily look good, cute, or appear "high speed."

Bandana and Shemagh

A bandana is small, lightweight, multipurpose, and full of utility. There is no reason not to have one and possible even two in your kit. A shemagh is a bit more bulky than a bandana but it is also lightweight, multipurpose, and full of utility. It is a must have due to the variety of uses it offers.

Sunglasses

Sunglasses are another must have item to protect your eyes from the sun and its damaging UV rays. If you are walking for long distances during the day your eyes can easily become fatigued from the bright sun. Sunglasses with UV protection is necessary. You can also obtain sunglasses that offer ballistic protection which will protect your eyes from damaging projectiles. This is a very worthwhile investment.

Goggles

Goggles are often neglected but serve a great purpose depending on the situation you may find yourself. First, you may be caught in the middle of a riot type situation or civil unrest. The police may resort to use of chemical agents for crowd control. Goggles can protect your eyes so that you can maintain your vision against the harmful effects of these chemical agents. If you have never experienced this situation take my advice and get goggles. Additionally, goggles can protect your eyes from the elements such as wind, sand storms, snow, dirt, and debris. Remember, an eye injury is a game changer and can stop you in your tracks. Even a small foreign object in the eye can cause significant problems and severe pain.

Bugging out in a severe dust storm is a serious hazard to your eyes. Googles are a great form of protection.

Pants

BDU style pants are a must in my opinion to carry items on your person in case you have to drop your bag and leave it behind. There is also a chance that a group of people may steal your bag. BDU style pants offer a lot of pockets to carry essential items on you in case you and your bag depart ways. Items that you must carry on you include: Wallet, prescription medication, knife, flashlight, cash, important phone numbers or information, map, etc.

Gloves

Gloves can offer significant protection of your hands which can take a lot of abuse during a bug out situation. Like your eyes and feet you want to take proper care of your hands. It is important to get gloves that fit your hands well and are not too big or small. A proper fit ensures not only protection of your hands but the ability to manipulate items and objects without significant loss of functionality or dexterity. I like to you use leather gloves by Mechanix as they fit great, are strong, and durable.

Rain Gear

It is better to be dry and comfortable (a relative term in a bug out situation) than wet and miserable. Being wet can make things more difficult and can be demoralizing. This is especially true if you become wet and cold. Therefore, it is good to have some type

Realistic Bug Out Bag

of protection from rain. It can be as simple as an inexpensive poncho or even a large garbage bag. If you choose you can opt for an expensive top of the line rain jacket from Arc'teryx, Marmot, Mountain Hardwear, Patagoina, or The North Face. The key is to stay dry especially in cold temperature where hypothermia can rapidly set in. While I normally say get the best gear you can afford I will state that there are many inexpensive ponchos that will work fine depending on where you live and the situation that you are dealing. They are not made of breathable material and do not come vented like quality jackets but they tend to work well. Having said that, if you live in an area that tends to get a lot of rain such as the pacific northwest then spend the money and get the best rain jacket that you can afford. This will be an investment that will be worth the cost of the jacket.

Max Cooper

Medical

Priorities should be on treating life-threatening injuries. When things go seriously south, injuries can come from many different sources and you must have the ability to provide enough treatment to keep yourself or family members alive as long as possible until further help is available. You may be faced with blunt force trauma, gunshot wounds, severe lacerations, avulsions, eviscerations, and amputations. Having the ability to rapidly assess these injuries and then provide a level of care that you are trained for can be the difference between life and death for that patient.

Consider the following questions:

- Do you know what to do for self-aid?
- Do you carry an Individual First Aid Kit (IFAK) on your person?
- Do you know how to stop profuse arterial bleeding?
- Do you carry a tourniquet on your person?
- Do you know how to improvise an effective tourniquet?
- Do you know how to treat an open "sucking" chest wound?
- Do you have the mindset to stay in the fight despite receiving severe injuries?

Realistic Bug Out Bag

Having the skill to perform self-aid or aid to a family member is critical. You cannot assume that during a crisis, even when in an urban environment, that medical care will be able to reach your location to provide aid. Never assume that first responders will be capable of helping you. It is incumbent upon you to be able to provide self-aid or family-aid until a higher level of care will be able to provide medical assistance. Having a medical kit is very important since the medical system to include hospitals and urgent care centers may be overwhelmed during the bug out event. In addition, first responders such as police, fire, and paramedics may be tied up with major incidents that are occurring. Many people will feel very vulnerable when they cannot pick up a phone and count on help to arrive. Most people in modern society have become overly reliant on the ability to call others for help. This has led to complacency and the inability to take care of oneself when necessary. The reality is that you may have to be self-reliant for an unknown period of time before medical care is available. Keep in mind that it does not take much for societies systems to become overwhelmed or completely break down.

Your kit must include any prescription medications that you take along with prescription eyewear to include glasses, contact lenses, and sunglasses. While your plan may be to bug out for 72 hours I recommend having a 10 day supply of any prescription medication just in case. If you have medicine that requires refrigeration you will need to have the ability to keep these meds in a cooler with ice. If you take prescription medication you should keep a list of the medication in your wallet. The list should include the following information:

- Name of the medication
- Dosage
- Directions for taking the medication
- Short description of the condition that the medication is used to treat
- RX number
- Name and phone number of doctor who prescribed medication
- Name and phone number of pharmacy
- Name of pharmacy insurance benefits with ID number and phone number
- Allergies to medication, food, or bites

Technically, you are supposed to carry prescription medication in the pill bottle that it came in with the label attached. But, in a bug out situation you may put them in a different carrier to save space. Having a sheet detailing your medication can be helpful if you become injured so that medical staff will have your prescription information along with any

Realistic Bug Out Bag

allergies that you have. Do this for each member of your family.

Your kit should include a supply of over the counter pain relievers, fever reducers, anti-diarrhea pills, ant-acids, anti-histamines, moleskin, a small assortment of bandages, tweezers, magnifying glass, etc.

Also include items that will treat significant trauma such as a tourniquet, hemostatic agent, chest seal, nasopharyngeal airway, etc. It is also important to have proper hands on training from a legitimate source for each of these items. Never provide care above your level of training.

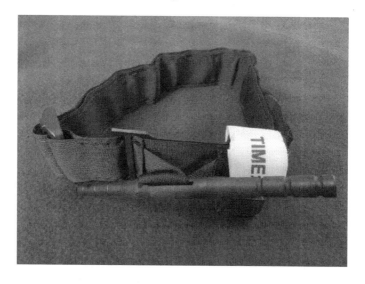

Combat Application Tourniquet (C-A-T)

The key is to balance the size of the medical kit so that it is not so big that it takes up too much room in your bug out bag. Only you can determine your "want" verse your "need" when it comes to your medical kit.

The IPOK with Combat Gauze is a good choice for treating a severe hemorrhage.

If you have allergies to medications, insect bites, food, or a chronic medical condition it is a good idea to have some type of medical alert tag that you wear on your wrist or neck. You can also attach a note to your driver's license.

One of the most important factors in relation to medical care is insuring that you have proper training to handle basic emergencies. At a minimum you should take a first aid/CPR/CCR/AED class which will

Realistic Bug Out Bag

provide you the basics. It will not make you a medical expert by any measure but it is important to have a rudimentary foundation on treating common injuries. It is also critical to remain calm during a crisis. If you lose control all those around you may lose control and the situation then spirals downward.

Two excellent books, along with their book descriptions, that I recommend are:

1. Trauma Care for the Worst Case Scenario by Gunner Morgan

    Book description[xi]:

    "Trauma Care for the Worst Case Scenario by Gunner Morgan covers medical considerations for dealing with serious injury resulting in severe bleeding or an open chest wound which are two leading causes of death from trauma such as gunshot, knife and blast injuries.  *Topics covered include: Types of emergency medical training, Tactical Combat Casualty Care applied to civilians, Individual First Aid Kit (IFAK) considerations, IFAK components to include a tourniquet, chest seal, pressure dressing, hemostatic agent, nasopharyngeal airways, and gloves; practical exercises and a list of useful resources."*

Max Cooper

2. Building a Trauma Kit by Gunner Morgan

Book description[xii]:

"Building a Trauma Kit by Gunner Morgan is the result of numerous requests from readers who read his successful book Trauma Care for the Worst Case Scenario. In Building a Trauma Kit Morgan goes over such factors as kit priorities, needs assessment, kit platform, components, medications, thoughts on wound suturing and more. This book is targeted for those interested in designing a high quality individualized kit. This is especially useful for preppers, concerned citizens, law enforcement officers, military personnel, correctional officers, detention officers, probation & parole officers, and others who want to know what to build a trauma kit for the worst case scenario. This book also covers components for a medical kit that covers emergency and non-emergency supplies. If you are not prepared for the Worst Case Scenario you are not prepared!"

I recommend these books because they have a practical and realistic approach to emergency medical situations that could become reality in a bug out situation. If you have prepared for the worst case situation you will be prepared for the best case situation. There are other books available on the subject although these two are very focused and on point.

Realistic Bug Out Bag

Keep in mind that regardless of what you carry you must know how to use each component in your kit. Not only must you have the knowledge and skills to provide care but you must be able to do it under great stress and potentially in an austere environment. Get training and be prepared. When seeking out training try to find a provider that offers scenario based training that is skill based and provides increasing levels of complexity.

Max Cooper

Weapons

Having a weapon in a bug out situation is a must. Unfortunately, it does not take much for society to break down and for people to tap into their evil side. People who are not grounded with a strong moral foundation can find themselves engaging in behaviors that are not typical. History is full of such horrific examples. When it comes to carrying a weapon the choice becomes what weapon are you legally allowed to carry in your area and what do you want to carry. At the end of the day, one of the best weapons to have is a firearm as it is the great equalizer. The problem with firearms is that they come with weight, bulk, and a lot of responsibility. Even in a bug out situation you may end up being held accountable to the law after the dust settles. Just about everyone has a cell phone with the ability to take photos and video. You may end up caught on such a tape that then becomes evidence against you in a court of law. Do not lose your ethics, morals, or humanity. Do not get sucked into the mob mentality. Even if you are never brought up on criminal charges you will be held accountable to your maker one day for your actions.

Firearm

We can debate which is the "best" firearm for the next hundred years and still not agree. Following is a truth that is hard to argue with:

Any firearm is better than no firearm when you need a firearm!

I will gladly take a .22 caliber pistol over nothing any day of the week. The firearm that I recommend is the Glock 19 with two spare magazines. This firearm has been around for years and while many people debate and criticize the 9mm round I have no problem with this caliber at all. Over the last 20 years there has been significant improvements in 9mm ballistics and I am fine with this round. I carried a 9mm on duty as a law enforcement officer for years and I stand by the Glock 19. The Glock is a very reliable, forgiving, and easy pistol to shoot. If you like a .45 caliber Colt then go for it. If you prefer a .38 caliber Smith & Wesson five shot revolver then go for it. Any "quality" firearm is better than none. The point is that you should have a firearm that you are trained to shoot, comfortable shooting, is reliable, and will go bang when you need it to fire. Remember, you can be held accountable and responsible for every round that leaves your barrel. You can also choose to carry a rifle or shotgun but remember that you are looking at more weight albeit more firepower.

Max Cooper

Glock 19, 9mm with skateboard tape on the top to help with one handed malfunction drills should I become injured. It works very well.

When it comes to firearms you must not only know how to properly and safety shoot the weapon but you must thoroughly know and understand tactics. This aspect of training is often neglected which is a huge mistake. Being able to hit your target accurately under stress is important but this is only one part of firearms skills. Unfortunately, a lot of individuals fail to train in tactics which is an extremely important component. If your firearms' training is held on a static range then you are not adequately prepared. If you think that playing paintball on the weekends is training you for real life violence then you are fooling yourself. Fortunately, there are now a lot of shooting schools that offer marksmanship, as well as, tactical training. This is one area that you really should spend the money and get quality training from a qualified instructor. Being able to hit a target on a static range is the foundation for you to build upon. Marksmanship is the basics and it is important to master the basics before moving on to more advanced skills. Do not rush to the sexy tactical training until you become very proficient with marksmanship.

In addition to proficient marksmanship skills you must train the following skills:

- The ability to shoot and move accurately
- Use cover and concealment
- Know how to clear malfunctions and be able to do it one handed if necessary
- Know the difference between shoot/no shoot situations
- Shoot in low-light conditions
- Know how to use a flashlight and/or laser
- Understand the use of light and shadows
- How to shoot and communicate
- How to maintain noise discipline
- Team tactics
- Structure clearing
- Downed person rescue

When you look at the above list, which is not necessarily a complete list, it should become clear that there is a lot more to shooting than standing on the 15 yard line and hitting a non-moving, non-threatening target that cannot shoot back and harm you. Obtaining proficient marksmanship and tactical skills requires time, consistency, discipline, patience, and practice. There are no shortcuts.

Knife

You will already have a fixed blade knife on you which can also function as a weapon with the added benefit of stealth. A knife can be silent and deadly. If you like you can also carry a tactical folder specifically as a weapon. There are literally hundreds of fighting knives to choose from ranging from inexpensive to very expensive, and high quality to no quality. Choose wisely. Remember, I recommend getting the best quality gear that you can afford. Some of the benefits of a tactical knife is that they are easy to carry, lightweight, easy to deploy, and very effective for inflicting damage. Like firearms, knives can also be very intimidating. They also require training to use as a self-defense weapon.

Walking Stick

Clearly a walking stick is designed for walking but can double as a weapon especially if you take time to get training in how to use it as a weapon. Also, some walking sticks are actually designed primarily as a weapon and just happen to double as a walking stick. Either way, a walking stick can be a very effective weapon in trained hands.

Pepper Spray

Pepper spray has been around for many years and is a good non-lethal choice. Pepper spray is also known as OC spray which is *Oleoresin Capsicum.* OC spray is classified as an inflammatory agent. When utilizing OC spray you want to target the face, nose, mouth, and eyes.

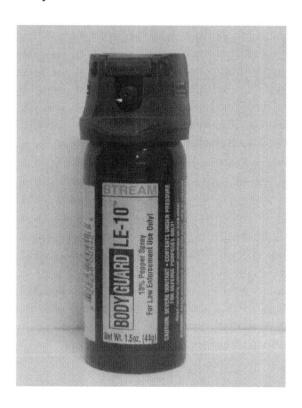

OC spray is a derivative of cayenne pepper. It produces involuntary closing of eyes known as a blepharospasm, impairs breathing as a result of uncontrollable coughing and gagging, intense burning to the skin, and temporary loss of muscular strength and coordination. It is most effective when inhaled and has a rapid onset of symptoms. It is effective for up to 45 minutes. Pepper spray is generally effective on animals, psychotic individuals and those under the influence of drugs and alcohol but nothing is 100% effective so have a backup plan.

Keep in mind that your environment will also have a host of weapons of opportunity. You just have to be aware of what is around you (situational awareness) and what you can potentially use as a weapon.

Realistic Bug Out Bag

Pets

If you own a pet you have an obligation to care for that pet during a crisis. It is not an option to leave your pet behind. If you feel it is safe enough to leave your pet at home then you need to stay home as well. Clearly, I view pets as part of the family and not an object. Pets rely on you 100% for their care and safety. When you get a pet you take on the responsibility to care for the pet all of the time. If you cannot accept this responsibility you should not own a pet. Abandonment of your pet is betrayal and unethical.

Pets must be included in your survival plan. Owning a pet(s) can severely increase the difficulty and complexity of your bug out situation. You need to provide water, food, shelter, medication if necessary, and all other pet care that is required. This will add to your weight and bulk. It may require that you have a specialized method of carrying items for your pet as you probably will not have room in your bug out bag.

Pets, especially dogs and cats, should be micro-chipped in case they become lost. Pets that are not micro-chipped who become lost and are then found by animal control are typically euthanized. This is preventable with a microchip and there is no excuse not to have all of your pets chipped. It is part of being a responsible pet owner.

Items to have for your dog include the following:

- Leash
- Collar with name tag and license tag. The name tag must include contact information
- Muzzle
- Backpack but keep in mind that you cannot overload the pack
- Food and water for three days to include a minimum of a ½ gallon of water per dog
- Food and water bowls
- Snacks / treats
- Any medications that your pet requires
- Booties for paw protection
- Sweater and/or blanket if needed
- Poop bags

It is highly advantageous that your pet, such as a dog, is trained and will listen to your commands. It is important that you carry veterinary contact information, as well as, vaccination and medical records with you. If you pet is allergic to food, medication, or bites you must have a medical alert tag on their collar.

Your dog is capable of wearing a pack but it must not be overloaded.

Max Cooper

If you suspect that your pet is poisoned you can contact the Pet Poison Helpline 24/7 at 800-213-6680. There is a $39 fee per incident. According to their website[xiii]:

> "Pet Poison Helpline is a 24-hour animal poison control service available throughout the U.S., Canada, and the Caribbean for pet owners and veterinary professionals who require assistance with treating a potentially poisoned pet. We have the ability to help every poisoned pet, with all types of poisonings, 24 hours a day. Our knowledge and expertise of pet poisons will put your mind at ease when dealing with a potential emergency.
>
> In order to provide this critical service, please be advised that there is a $39 per incident fee, payable by credit card. This fee covers the initial consultation as well as all follow-up calls associated with the management of the case."

During a crisis that requires you to bug out it is important to realize that many shelters will not accept pets. This reality limits your options and increases the complexity of your situation. Attempt to find emergency animal hospitals and shelters that will take animals during a crisis. This can provide you with peace of mind knowing that your animals have a safe place to go assuming that you are capable of getting to the location.

Realistic Bug Out Bag

Miscellaneous Items

This can be a wide open category so keep your "needs" a priority and separate them from your "wants" which will quickly burden you with weight and bulk. Try to limit miscellaneous items to individualized needs, environmental needs, and medical issues. Avoid comfort items when possible which are really wants and not needs. The exception to this is hygiene and when you have young children or older adults.

Technically there is no right or wrong items to carry. There are just items that take up space and add weight. You are going to be the person carrying your gear so it is you who will pay the price if you overload your bug out bag. Ultimately, your kit and your gear is your responsibility. Test it out prior to a bug out situation to find what works and what does not work.

This section is not going to cover every possible item that can go in your bug out bag as the list would be very long and quite frankly many of the lists that I see are comprised of "filler" items that offer no real benefit. I am including items that may (or may not) be useful to you. Only you will know the individualized factors that pertain to your needs. Choose wisely and always keep weight in mind.

Max Cooper

Map and Compass

In some respect the need to have a map and compass may not be as important as some people advocate. The reason is that you *should* have practiced your plan numerous times and know the location, routes, and contingency plans for your bug out. Yet, even then it is a great idea to have a map and compass for one simple reason…plans change. The only time a map and compass is not necessary is when everything works out as you planned but this is rarely ever the case. Be prepared for every eventuality and a map and compass is an invaluable tool. It is also a great idea to get satellite or aerial photos of the area that you will be in as this can provide useful intelligence especially when dealing with an urban area. Keep in mind that the photos may not be current so use the photos with caution.

In regards to GPS units I do not advocate carrying one for numerous reasons. First, batteries will eventually die. Even in a 72 hour bug out you may find yourself burning through batteries depending on how much you use your unit. Second, depending on the situation the government has the capability to prevent civilians from receiving GPS signals making your unit worthless. Third, they weigh more than a map and compass!

Personal Hygiene

Even for a short bug out of 72 hours it is important to take personal hygiene seriously to prevent the spread of germs and to make you feel better. Fortunately, many of the items that you should consider carrying are small and lightweight. I recommend a toothbrush, small tube of toothpaste, disinfecting wipes, hand sanitizer, and dental floss. The simple act of being able to wipe off your face with disinfecting wipes and brushing your teeth can make you feel human again after a long brutal day of walking. Always clean hands before eating to prevent any contamination of food that could lead to a foodborne illness. If you don't have access to soap and water use hand sanitizer. According to the CDC[xiv]:

*"Washing hands with soap and water is the best way to reduce the number of microbes on them in most situations. If soap and water are not available, use an alcohol-based hand sanitizer that contains at least 60% alcohol. Alcohol-based hand sanitizers can quickly reduce the number of microbes on hands in some situations, but sanitizers do **not** eliminate all types of germs."*

Duct Tape

Duct tape is one of those items that is a necessity as it is so useful for many tasks. Wrap a bunch around a credit card and it will be compact, lightweight, and very versatile. There are just too many valuable uses for duct tape not to have some with you. The most effective duct tape that I have found is Gorilla Brand. This is the brand that I use and recommend. Avoid silver or grey duct tape which is too visible and reflective.

Walking Stick

A walking stick can be a valuable asset because it can function in multiple roles. In addition to helping you walk and maintain your stability, a quality walking stick, depending on the material, can function as a self-defense weapon and it can help with building a shelter. A lot of people make their own walking stick out of a very strong wood and add items such as a small button compass and even a fishing kit that is placed in a hollowed out portion of the handle. You can also wrap paracord on the handle to help with your grip and this will provide extra rope if necessary. A walking stick is something to seriously consider.

Realistic Bug Out Bag

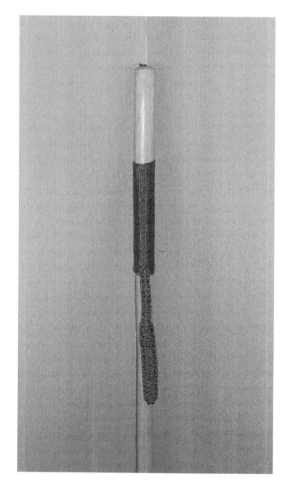

Wood walking stick with Paracord wrapped handle that can also function as a weapon.

Binoculars/Monocular

Having the ability to see distant objects can be a very valuable asset in a bug out situation especially if society is breaking down and acts of violence are occurring. The ability to gather intelligence from a distance should not be taken lightly. Fortunately, there are a lot of options available that are relatively small and lightweight making this a viable option to add to your bug out kit. It is also important to remember that if you are bugging out on foot you should be scanning your environment all of the time. This not only includes what is in front of you but each side, behind you and when applicable above and below you. Situational awareness means knowing what is occuring in a 360 degree sphere. Remember, you cannot respond to a potential problem if you are not aware of the problem. Situational awareness helps to prevent you from being blindsided.

Zip Ties

There are generally two types of zip ties and each one is very different:

1. Those used by law enforcement

2. Those used to bind small objects like cords together sometimes referred to as heavy duty cable ties

It is a good idea to carry both types with you as they are small and lightweight. Some use the heavy duty cable ties to secure individuals but they were not designed for this purpose and they are relatively easy to defeat and break free. There are many YouTube videos demonstrating how easy it is to defeat these types of zip ties. The ones designed for law enforcement use, on the other hand, are much more difficult to escape from or defeat. It is important to use the proper tool for the proper job. Heavy duty cable ties are not designed to secure people.

Zip ties offer a lot of utility in a small package and can be very helpful. Like many aspects of survival it comes down to your creativity in seeing how such items can be utilized. Zip ties can be used in building a shelter, securing items together, attaching an item to your backpack, fixing broken gear, putting up a tarp, etc.

Whistle

If you have children or elderly individuals with you then a whistle is a great piece of gear to carry especially if the person becomes lost or separated from the group. Using a whistle is easier and requires much less energy than yelling or screaming. You can also have a covert means of communicating with a whistle. Personally, I like the JetScream whistle as it is flat, small, and loud. You can get it in bright orange or black depending on your needs. There is no reason not to carry a whistle.

JetScream Whistle with integrated compass and paracord lanyard. I put this together in less than half an hour.

Signal Mirror

This is another item that is very small, lightweight, durable, and multi-functional. You can use it for signaling purposes, as a mirror, or to start a fire by reflecting the sun on a focal point. In some environments a signal mirror can be seen from miles away. As a fire starter I would resort to using a signal mirror as one of my last options way behind a lighter, firesteel and matches.

Hand & Foot Warmers

In cold and wet weather hand and foot warmers can provide an excellent level of comport from the biting cold. They are small, lightweight, effective, inexpensive, come in a variety of sizes, last a long time, and they work. Every member of your family should have some warmers in their bug out bag. Some even come with a protective cover to prevent burns.

When using warmers use some caution with younger children because these can get too hot. Also, use caution with the elderly who may have blood flow issues from diabetes or other medical problems. In cold weather these hand warmers are great to have especially when you stop for the day and the cold grips you.

Mask

A mask such as a N95 mask can provide protection from debris in the air which can trigger a respiratory problem. Natural disasters and acts of terrorism can wreak having on the environment and fill the air with a lot of harmful debris. This was very evident during the terrorist attacks of 9/11. This is a product that really requires some research to find a mask that best fits your needs. Masks come in many different varieties from small and inexpensive to large, fitted, and more expensive. When possible you are best served by obtaining a fitted mask that will fit your face better and offer an increased level of protection. I highly recommend that you obtain a mask that is certified by the National Institute for Occupational Safety and Health (NIOSH) which is the U.S. Government agency responsible for the certification and approval of respiratory protective devices for occupational use.

Following is information from the Centers for Disease Control (CDC) on respirators[xv]:

What is a respirator?

A respirator is a personal protective device that is worn on the face, covers at least the nose and mouth, and is used to reduce the wearer's risk of inhaling hazardous airborne particles (including dust particles and infectious agents), gases, or vapors. Respirators are considered as a "last line of defense" in the occupational hierarchy of controls. They are recommended when engineering and administrative controls are not feasible or sufficient to control the hazard, or until these other controls can be put in place.

Respirators protect the user in two basic ways; either by filtering contaminated ambient air or by providing a clean source of air. Respirators that remove contaminants from the air are called air-purifying respirators (APRs). APRs include particulate respirators, which filter out airborne particles, and "gas masks," which remove gasses and vapors from ambient air.

The classification of air-purifying respirators can be further subdivided into three categories:

1. Filtering facepiece respirators (FFRs) – Sometimes referred to as disposable particulate respirators because the entire respirator is discarded when it becomes unsuitable for further use due to considerations of hygiene, excessive resistance, or physical damage. These are also commonly referred to as "N95s."

2. Elastomeric facepiece respirators – Sometimes referred to as reusable respirators because the facepiece is cleaned and reused while the filter cartridges and canisters are discarded and replaced when they become unsuitable for further use.

3. Powered air-purifying respirators (PAPRs) – A battery-powered blower moves the air through the filters to the user.

Max Cooper

The other types of respirators, which protect by supplying clean air from another source are called air-supplying respirators (ASRs). This type of respirator is comprised of airline, or supplied air, respirators (SARs), which use compressed air from a remote source; and self-contained breathing apparatuses (SCBAs), which include their own breathing gas (compressed air or oxygen) supply.

What is an N95 respirator?

The NIOSH respiratory protection approval regulation (42 CFR 84) defines the term "N95" to refer to a filter class, not a respirator. However, many filtering facepiece respirators have an N95 class filter and many people refer to them, and have come to know them, as N95 respirators. A filtering facepiece respirator that filters out at least 95% of airborne particles during "worse case" testing using a "most-penetrating" sized particle is given a 95 rating. There are nine classes of NIOSH-approved particulate filtering respirators available at this time. 95% is the minimal level of filtration that will be approved by NIOSH.

Window Punch

A window punch is designed to break safety glass typically found in automobiles. During a bug out situation a window punch may come in handy. They are small, inexpensive, and generally very effective. I have used these on multiple automobile windows and they all shattered with ease. The window will shatter but you will still need to remove the glass to enter into the vehicle. Whenever you break glass take extra precaution not to get cut or punctured. The last thing you need is a serious cut or an injury that becomes infected. One hasty decision or rushed action can lead to a serious injury.

Water Key

In an urban environment a water key is very handy for outside water faucets that are typically found in the back of strip mall stores and other public locations such as parks and playgrounds. This key generally comes with multiple sizes and are capable of turning on a water faucet. They often come in the following standard sizes: 1/4" - 9/32" and 5/16" - 11/32"

During a bug out event this key may provide you access to life saving water. At a minimum, it may provide you the opportunity to top off your water supply. The key is very small, lightweight, and inexpensive. Well worth having during a crisis. If the water from the faucet does not appear to be clean you may need to resort to boiling or using other methods to make the water drinkable to avoid getting sick. Look at and smell the water before drinking to see if you notice any signs that the water may not be drinkable. If you are not sure take appropriate measure to make the water safe.

Waterproof Bags

Waterproof bags can come in handy to protect valuable electronic equipment such as cell phones and radios or to keep your clothes dry. There are a lot of options with waterproof bags and pouches. They tend to be very lightweight and you will appreciate the protection they provide especially in inclement weather. I have used Aloksak Bags by LOKSAK and they tend to work well. There are also waterproof cases that you can use in conjunction with a waterproof bag if you are looking for an extra layer of protection.

Permanent Marker

This is a great item to have if you need to link up with your group at a predesignated meeting place and then determine that it is not safe and you need to go to your secondary location. You can use your permanent marker to leave a visible note for your party to see. I would carry one in the color black and one that is red. If necessary, you can come up with a simple code that only members of your group will understand. If you decide to use a code keep it very simple and easy to understand under stressful situations.

Survival Candles

In an urban environment you really need to be careful with any form of fire especially if there is potential for a gas leak. Burning a candle can make a bad situation much worse. But, if you are sure that you are in a safe area a survival candle that burns up to 9 hours is a good idea. They are lightweight, compact, and inexpensive. You can even buy a holder that will secure the candle to increase your level of safety to prevent an accidental fire. Always be extremely careful with fire especially around children and the elderly. Do NOT burn candles inside of a tent which is a recipe for disaster.

Lock Picks

Lock picks can be a valuable item especially in an urban setting but they are not without risk and I am not referring to legal risk. If you enter a place that is inhabited you may end up looking down the barrel of a handgun, rifle, or shotgun. Also, while lock picking is not necessarily a difficult skill to learn it does take practice. Only carry a lock pick set if you are actually proficient with picking locks AND you have a reason to carry them in a bug out situation. Do not carry a set just to have it. Carry it for a specific reason and have the skill to use it effectively.

Hearing Protection

Hearing protection in the form of earplugs can be a very valuable asset although they can also be a double edged sword. If the environment is very loud you may resort to the use of hearing protection. Yet, they also limit your ability to hear sounds that can directly impact your safety. You never want to lose situational awareness during a crisis. There are electronic earmuffs used for shooters that block out loud sounds but can allow other sounds through so that you can hear. These can be expensive and a little bulky but they are an option. Hearing protection is also good for children and the elderly who can easily become frightened by loud noises. Hearing protection can provide a layer of perceived comfort and protection.

Notebook and Pen

Having a notebook and writing instrument can be extremely valuable items to have during your bug out. Besides providing you the ability to write notes to give to others it is a great idea to document your situation. For the majority of people a bug out situation is a very rare event but from past experience we know that it can and does happen. It would be a good idea each night, as you wind down, to write an informal report of:

- What went well
- What did not go well
- What modifications need to occur
- Ideas to plan for future situations
- Lessons learned
- Injuries, medical conditions received
- Threats encountered
- Weather and environmental factors

It is important to write down your ideas as soon as possible because you do not want to forget valuable nuggets of information that will benefit you or others in the future.

Carabineer

When referring to a carabineer I do not mean the toy kind that is used to hold keys. I mean a carabineer that is designed for weight bearing. Because they tend to be small and lightweight you can carry more than one depending on your needs.

Flare Gun

Carrying a flare gun in your bug out bag is a rather unique option yet it might be one that comes in handy. For example, if you are in an area where the power grid is down and you need illumination for scouting purposes a flare gun is a viable option. Also, if you are in an area that is potentially turning violent, utilization of a flare gun *may* make some of the bad people believe that there is police presence. Of course you cannot assume this to be the case but it may cause some to seek the dark like cockroaches. It is no guarantee but it is an option and options are good to have during a bug out. A flare gun can also aid in rescue situations if you need assistance. While it can be done I do not recommend using a flare gun as a method to start a fire unless you know what you are doing.

Batteries

It is not uncommon for much of the equipment in your gear setup to take batteries. One way to maintain efficiency, cost effectiveness, and weight reduction is to, when possible; standardize your batteries so that all, or most, of your equipment uses the same size battery. This will allow you to interchange your batteries if necessary. Depending on your needs this may not always be possible. There will always be a cost/benefit ratio that you must contend with and see if you can live with the advantages and disadvantages. There is a lot of technology that goes into producing batteries. I am purposefully going to stay away from the details and minutia so not as to bore you.

As for me, I have made the conscious decision to stay away from CR123 lithium batteries if at all possible. I realize that this means that when using AA or AAA lithium batteries I sacrifice power (voltage) but I also reap the benefits of less expensive batteries, longer run-times, more availability, and most important the ability to use the batteries in different pieces of gear.

I completely understand that CR123 lithium batteries have more output for high-demand pieces of gear and can offer higher voltages than your standard AA lithium battery. But, how often do we need such high output especially when CR123 batteries are more expensive, have relatively short runtimes, and have less availability? If you work in law enforcement, the military, security, and other such jobs then you may justify the added expense. When my life is potentially on the line I never sacrifice cost. And, neither should you.

Another option to consider is rechargeable batteries. Typically the up-front cost is more expensive but they can be used over and over again. Many can be recharged using solar panel kits which are small enough to carry with you. Be sure to read the instructions of the electronic devices that you have because some of them state not to use rechargeable batteries. Having used different brands of rechargeable batteries the brand that I prefer and carry are Eneloop.

Max Cooper

Benefits of <u>Lithium AA and AAA</u> Batteries:

- ➲ The lithium AA and AAA battery can be found almost anywhere

- ➲ This level of availability is its greatest strengths

- ➲ These batteries are also very lightweight

- ➲ Are an adequate performer for most of your needs even in a bug out situation

- ➲ More cost efficient compared to CR123 lithium batteries but more expensive than AA or AAA alkaline batteries

- ➲ Work well in extreme temperatures

- ➲ Long shelf life

Disadvantages of <u>Lithium AA and AAA</u> Batteries:

- More expensive than alkaline batteries

- Less power output

Realistic Bug Out Bag

Benefits of <u>Lithium CR123</u> Batteries:

- ⮊ Higher voltage output resulting in more power

- ⮊ Ability to have smaller sized and more powerful flashlights

- ⮊ Long shelf life

Disadvantages of <u>Lithium CR123</u> Batteries:

- Expensive

- Not widely available

- There have been a lot of counterfeit CR123 batteries flooding the market. Some of these batteries have exploded leading to severe injuries.

Benefits of <u>Rechargeable</u> Batteries:

- ⮊ Inexpensive over the long haul

- ⮊ Long life and can often be recharged anywhere from 1,000-1,500 times

- ⮊ Can be charged with a solar power unit

Max Cooper

Disadvantages of <u>Rechargeable</u> Batteries:

- Can have an up-front cost for the batteries and charger

- Eventually they will not be able to be recharged

- Not all electrical devices will accept rechargeable batteries

The good news is that battery technology is rapidly advancing so my thoughts may change as battery technology improves. Overall, lithium batteries are much better than alkaline batteries. Following is the way I use batteries in my electronic equipment. Depending on the equipment I will initially use either AA or AAA lithium batteries such as Energizer. Once those batteries go dead I will switch to using Eneloop rechargeable batteries. My reasoning for doing this is because the lithium batteries typically last a long time. Once they are dead I will throw them out which now reduces my weight. Remember, weight adds up so any opportunity to get rid of something is a benefit. I realize lithium batteries are light but every little bit helps. And, it saves a little bit of space.

Never underestimate the ability to interchange batteries between different items of gear. This is especially true during a crisis when you may not have the opportunity to get to a store to obtain more batteries or other equipment. If you have already invested a lot of money in gear that uses CR123 batteries don't worry as your investment is not a waste. But, as you begin to build, modify your setup, and analyze your gear you can now begin to integrate items that use a more standardized type of battery. Also, there are many people who will be willing to trade gear. There are many "uninformed" consumers of gear who will gladly trade up to a CR123 flashlight because of the added power output while not thinking of the disadvantages. Their lack of knowing and understanding the advantages and disadvantages of gear can be used to your benefit.

Children and the Elderly

This is a category that can be very varied depending on the age of the individuals involved, their physical and mental capabilities, medical conditions, and level of training. One of the biggest pieces of advice that I can offer when dealing with children and the elderly is to be patient. Getting frustrated or upset will not make a bad situation any better. In fact, it can make it significantly worse.

Children

Children need to feel a level of safety and security at all times. Even if the situation is bad it is extremely important for parents to remain strong and display an air of confidence that all is well. Do not lie to your children but you do not have to tell them everything. Provide information that is age appropriate. This can be challenging especially when things are not going well. But, if your children do not feel safe they may excessively worry, completely shut down, or potentially act out. Each of these situations may distract you from doing what is necessary to safely lead your family to a better situation. Never forget that your children are looking up to you, as their parent, to make everything better. If you cannot remain composed neither will your children. Panic can be contagious and so can calmness. Remain cool, calm, and collected if only for the benefit of your children.

Push your children too hard or make their bug out bag too heavy and this is what will happen...kid down!

Realistic Bug Out Bag

Bring things that will keep your children occupied especially during down time. This can include small games, books, electronic items with extra batteries, music with headphones, a favorite stuffed animal etc. Also, give your children age appropriate responsibilities or have them help out when possible. Keep their minds active so they do not have time to think about the situation. Even if you provide small easy tasks they will feel as if they are contributing. This will build their confidence, self-esteem, and value to the family. It is especially important that as a parent you be extra patient and not yell or be critical of your child(ren) as this will significantly make a bad situation much worse. As a parent you need to step up and be a strong leader for your family. Your whole family needs you to be strong and confident even if you are terrified on the inside.

Elderly

Elderly individuals provide a host of other potential issues. As with young children the elderly need to feel safe. Elderly individuals may not be as physically strong or mental sharp as they were in their youth. They may have multiple medical conditions that need to be considered. This can lead to feeling unsafe or that they are a burden to you, your family, or the group. Be sure to bring all medications, glasses, or other medical equipment such as braces. Remember, with age comes wisdom. Regularly ask for their input and advice to make them feel like they are contributing. When possible, provide elderly individuals with tasks that they are capable of completing. Do not overwhelm them as they may not be able to handle stress very well. As people age their ability to effectively handle stress can diminish. Make them feel as a valued and productive part of the group without taxing their capabilities. As with children be extra patient.

There are so many variables that arise with children and the elderly that you must really consider the possibilities ahead of time and plan accordingly. In fact, you may come to the conclusion that bugging out is not an option in which case you need a "bug in" plan that will permit you to survive the situation. Unfortunately, there may be times when you are left with a situation where you have to choose from a list of options that are not so appealing. Always do what is best for your family.

Bicycle or Tricycle

Now this is taking the "miscellaneous" category in a whole new direction. No, you are not going to be carrying your bike. Technically it is a form of transportation and not an item in your gear. Even the lightest bike is too heavy and bulky to carry. But, if you live in an area that is very congested or the roads are going to end up in gridlock then a bike is a viable option.

I recommend using a mountain bike as they are generally well built and very capable on different types of terrain. I suggest that you get a high quality front light and a rear light if you want to travel at night. When possible get tubeless bike tires. They are more costly but provide a great option. You can look up these tires at www.notubes.com. If the cost is too prohibitive get thorn proof tires to try and help prevent flats. I use thorn proof tires and still get flats more often that I like. Carry a tire patch kit, spare tube, and a small pump that can be attached to the bike frame. Changing a bike tire in the middle of a crisis is not a good situation. It is also important to keep your bike well maintained on a regular basis so it is ready to go at a moment's notice.

The benefits of traveling on bike include:

- You can travel much <u>faster</u> than on foot. Even if you were only able to travel at 10 miles per hour on bike you can still cover a lot of distance fairly quickly.
- You can travel <u>further</u>. At 10mph you can cover 20 miles in only 2 hours which

is much further than what you can do on foot.
- Can go places that a car cannot travel
- Quiet form of transportation when noise discipline is important which can be extremely important if violence is occuring
- Does not require an outside form of fuel just human power
- You can potentially hook up a small bike trailer to haul extra items but remember this will require that you use more energy
- If you are with a group it can be possible for one or two members to scout out the road and conditions about a ½ mile ahead of the group. They can report back through radio communications using a FRS/GMRS radio. Remember, radio channels may be very busy and nothing that you say over the radio is private. It is best to keep communications short and clear.

Realistic Bug Out Bag

FRS/GMRS radios from Motorola and Midland.

- If you have the technical skill you can harvest the power from pedaling to power your electronic items or to recharge such items.

There are also some potential negatives from riding a bike as your mode of bug out transportation:

- Burns a lot of calories which can increase your food requirements
- Can be physically exhausting
- Offers no protection from the elements
- Not every member of your group may be able to ride do to health reasons or lack of physical conditioning
- Leaves you open and potentially vulnerable
- Can lead to injuries if a member crashes
- May not be possible due to road conditions or environmental factors
- Can encounter a mechanical failure that is not fixable in the field
- May be difficult to ride a bike while wearing your bug out bag as your center of gravity may become unstable

If you choose to use a bike as a form of transportation you will need to know how to do basic maintenance such as changing a flat tire. You also have to be willing to either ditch the bike or hide it when necessary if the road conditions become too difficult or for another reason. This can result in the loss of a lot of money. And, there is always the possibility that people will "bike-jack" you and steal your bike.

Another option is a tricycle which should also be considered as a bug out mode of transportation. A tricycle may not be as mobile or able to go where a bicycle can but it can still serve a very valuable purpose.

Benefits include:

- Increased level of stability. A tricycle offers stability because it has three wheels and not two. This can be important especially if you have medical conditions such as vertigo or you become tired and need extra stability.

- Increased space for cargo which will allow you to bring more items with you. Do not overload the cargo area because it is still going to require that you pedal the trike which burns valuable calories. The goal is to still remain light and mobile. If you decide to use a trailer keep in mind that it can limit your ability to negotiate difficult terrain.

- Ability to carry passengers which can allow you to transport young children, elderly individuals, pets, or an injured/exhausted person. Keep in mind that as the weight goes up so does the amount of energy that you expend. If you are not in excellent physical condition you may end up exhausted in a very short period of time. When possible, take turns so that one person is not the main form of power. Share the pain! This is an added benefit of having multiple people in your group especially if everyone is in excellent physical condition.

- You could potentially hook up a small motor and carry some extra fuel. This will allow you to carry heavier items. But, you must also realize that if/when you run out of fuel or the motor becomes inoperable then you will need to pedal the tricycle. If the weight is too heavy you may need to off load some items possibly including the motor.

Realistic Bug Out Bag

Summary

The focus of this book has been on your bug out bag but one very important item that has not been discussed, which is critical, is your survival plan. It is absolutely necessary to have a written plan. At a minimum, your plan should include:

- Contact information for different people such as family, friends, and your network
- Out of state contacts
- List of other important phone numbers
- Rally points to meet family, friends, and your network that include primary, secondary, and tertiary locations
- Multiple routes to your bug out location that include vehicle and foot routes
- Communication plan
- Contingency plans
- Map of local area
- List of area hospitals, fire stations, and police stations
- Plan for your pets
- Plan for children and/or elderly

- Also, have written goals for any areas that you need to work on and improve

Keep in mind that the heavier your bug out bag is the slower you will travel and the more likely you are to obtain an injury. Remember, the goal is to be **light**, **mobile**, and **efficient** which will mean that you are also faster. But, you can only be as fast as the slowest member of your team. There are so many variables to bugging out that it can be a constant struggle to keep your pack light. This is especially true if you are responsible for family. If you are on your own you will have a lot less to consider.

When choosing items to place into your bug out bag ask yourself the following questions:

1. Is the item a *want* or a *need*?
2. Does it perform multiple functions?
3. Is the quality acceptable and reliable?
4. Do I know how to properly use the item?
5. Is the item good weight or bad weight?
6. Are there alternative items that are better and/or lighter?
7. Do you have redundant items?

A heavy emphasis is placed on weight because you will quickly feel the impact of a heavy pack which can slow you down or lead to injury. **Do not fall into the trap of letting your *perceived* ability exceed your *actual* ability.** The truth will eventually come out. You can deny reality for only so long before it bites you in the rear. If you have tested yourself as I have recommended earlier there is zero chance that you will fall into this trap. This means that you will be more prepared than the average person who chooses not to test themselves or their gear. This is a huge mistake that will have consequences.

Hopefully you will never be in a situation that requires you to bug out. But, it is comforting to know that, if you have completely prepared, you are ready by having the following:

- Primary plan
- Contingency plan
- Bug out bag
- Necessary physical fitness
- Proper mental preparation

There is something to be said for having peace of mind knowing that you are ready at a moment's notice. If you do have to bug out it is important to be flexible and adaptable to a potentially austere situation that is dynamic and full of unknown factors. It will not be easy or comfortable even when you are prepared. It will be hell if you are not prepared. It will also be too late and you will have to do the best you can with what you are capable of doing under the circumstances. As the saying goes, *"Failing to prepare, is preparing to fail."* You and your family deserve better so prepare.

Remember, it is virtually impossible for any book to cover every potential variable that you may encounter. It is an unrealistic expectation of the reader to believe this to be possible. This is why I have stressed that you, as the reader, should take what you can use and discard the rest. Apply what is applicable to your situation. Ultimately, planning for a bug out, or a "bug in" situation, is completely your responsibility. It is you and/or your family or group members that will pay the price for your failures. The buck stops with you. This is a huge responsibility so take the time to plan, prepare, train, test, and modify your set up on a regular basis. The process does not end. This is a huge and important responsibility. This is especially crucial since your knowledge base will expand and grow over time, new items of gear will come to market, your children will grow and be able to take on more responsibilities, etc. Life is very dynamic which requires that you constantly need to re-evaluate your plans and your bug out bag. Your bug out bag is not a set it and forget it item. Also keep in mind that unused items will periodically need to be replaced. As you can see there are a lot of factors and variable that go into a bug out bag. Only you will know what is required for your situation.

The last point that I would like to make is that there are a lot of books available about bug out bags. It is interesting to see comments that the book is "too basic." I will agree that there are a lot of books that offer little to no insightful information. But, I think it is incorrect to view such books as basic or advanced. In reality the information:

- Is either useful or it is not

- Provides a new or unique perspective or it does not

There really is no such thing as an "advanced" bug out bag. There is only information that applies to your situation or it does not. Your bug out bag either works for your situation or it does not. Do not look to over complicate your situation.

It is my hope that you have found a few relevant nuggets of information that will benefit you in your journey of preparing a bug out bag. If you consider yourself an expert and already have a bug out bag built to your individualized needs I highly recommend that, at a minimum, you test your gear by conducting the 10, 15, and 20 mile hike that I talked about earlier. This exercise will really tell you a lot about your bug out bag, your physical conditioning, and your mental toughness. Finally, remember that every item you choose to place in your bug out bag has a cost/benefit ratio associated with the piece of gear. Choose wisely...very wisely.

Good luck, stay safe, prepare, train, modify as needed and be strong. Failure is not an option.

I can be contacted at:

maximum.cooper@cox.net

Resources

Books:

- *How to Set Goals and Keep Them* by Scott Kirshner, M.Ed.

- *Trauma Care for the Worst Case Scenario* by Gunner Morgan

- *Building a Trauma Kit* by Gunner Morgan

- *Amateur Radio Service: Part 97* by Kent Hertz

- *Emergency Radio Communications* by Caleb Watts

- *Principles of Personal Defense* by Jeff Cooper

- *MindSighting: Mental Toughness Skills for Police Officers in High Stress Situations* by Michael J. Asken

- *Unleash the Warrior Within* by Richard Machowicz

- *Combative Fundamentals: An Unconventional Approach* by Jeff Gonzales

- *The Gift of Fear* by Gavin de Becker

- ***The Strategies of Low-Light Engagements*** by Ken Good

- ***Training at the Speed of Life*** by Kenneth R. Murray

Realistic Bug Out Bag

Knives:

- Benchmade   http://www.benchmade.com/
- Buck Knives   http://www.buckknives.com/
- Cold Steel   http://www.coldsteel.com/
- ESEE   http://www.eseeknives.com/
- Gerber   http://www.gerbergear.com/
- Ka-Bar   http://www.kabar.com/
- Kershaw   http://www.coldsteel.com/
- Leatherman   http://www.leatherman.com/
- Mora   http://www.moraofsweden.se/
- Ontario   http://ontarioknife.com/
- SOG   https://www.sogknives.com/
- Spyderco   http://www.spyderco.com/
- Swiss Army   http://www.swissarmy.com/us

Fire:

- BIC Lighter	http://www.biclighter.com/
- Coghlans	http://www.coghlans.com/
- Exotac	http://www.exotac.com/
- Light My Fire	http://www.lightmyfire.com/
- Live Fire	http://www.livefiregearllc.com/
- Stormproof Matches http://www.industrialrev.com/
- Ultimate Survival Technology

    http://www.ultimatesurvival.com/

- Zippo	http://www.zippo.com/

Realistic Bug Out Bag

Water:

- Aquamira — http://www.aquamira.com/
- Camelbak — http://www.camelbak.com/
- Geigerrig — http://www.geigerrig.com/
- Guyot Designs — https://www.guyotdesigns.com/
- Katadyn — http://www.katadyn.com/usen/
- LifeStraw — http://www.buylifestraw.com/
- Miox — http://www.miox.com/
- Nalgene — http://nalgene.com/
- Nuun — http://www.nuun.com/
- PlatyPus — http://www.cascadedesigns.com/
- Potable Aqua — http://www.potableaqua.com/
- Sawyer — http://sawyer.com/
- SteriPEN — http://www.steripen.com/
- Vitalyte — http://www.vitalyte.com/

Food:

- Backpackers Pantry
  https://www.backpackerspantry.com/
- Clif Bars   http://www.clifbar.com/
- Datrex   http://www.datrex.com/
- Esbit Stoves   http://www.esbit.de/en
- Fish Pouches   https://www.starkist.com/
- GU Energy Gel   https://guenergy.com/
- Hammer Nutrition
  http://www.hammernutrition.com/
- Jerky   http://www.jacklinks.com/
- Mountain House http://www.mountainhouse.com/
- Nutriom   http://www.nutriom.com/#all-natural-egg-crystals
- Power Bar   http://www.powerbar.com/
- Pro Bar   http://shop.theprobar.com/
- Trail Mix   http://www.planters.com/
- Wise Company   https://wisefoodstorage.com/

Realistic Bug Out Bag

Shelter:

- Adventure Medical Kits
    https://www.adventuremedicalkits.com/
- Blizzard Survival

    http://www.blizzardsurvival.com/
- Chinook   http://www.chinooktec.com/
- ENO
    http://www.eaglesnestoutfittersinc.com/
- Grabber   http://grabberworld.com/
- Hennessy   http://hennessyhammock.com/
- Kammok   http://kammok.com/
- Marmot   http://marmot.com/
- Proforce
    http://www.proforceequipment.com/
- REI   http://www.rei.com/
- Terra Nova   http://www.terra-nova.co.uk/
- Therm-A-Rest   http://www.cascadedesigns.com/

Light:

- Black Diamond   http://blackdiamondequipment.com/
- Cyalume   http://www.cyalume.com/
- EagleTac   http://www.eagletac.com/
- Fenix   http://www.fenixlight.com/
- JETBeam   http://www.jetbeamlighting.com/
- Maratac   http://countycomm.com/
- Petzl   http://www.petzl.com/us
- Princeton Tec   http://www.princetontec.com/
- Streamlight   http://www.streamlight.com/en-us
- SureFire   http://www.surefire.com/

Realistic Bug Out Bag

Communication:

- Ambient Weather

    http://www.ambientweather.com/
- Eton   http://www.etoncorp.com/en
- Icom   http://www.icomamerica.com/en/
- Kaito   http://www.kaitousa.com/
- Kenwood   http://www.kenwoodusa.com/
- Midland   https://midlandusa.com/
- Panasonic   http://www.panasonic.com/
- Sangean

    http://www.sangean.com/first/first.asp
- Sony   http://www.sony.com/
- Yaesu   http://www.yaesu.com/

Clothing:

- 5.11 Tactical   http://www.511tactical.com/
- Adidas   http://www.adidas.com/us/
- Arc'teryx   http://arcteryx.com/
- Columbia   http://www.columbia.com/
- Lowa   http://www.lowaboots.com/
- Marmot   http://marmot.com/
- Mountain Hardware   http://www.mountainhardwear.com/
- Patagonia   http://www.patagonia.com/
- Revision Military   https://www.revisionmilitary.com/
- Saloman   http://www.salomon.com/us/
- SmartWool   http://www.smartwool.com/
- The North Face   http://www.thenorthface.com/
- Tilley   http://www.tilley.com/
- Under Armor   http://www.underarmour.com/
- Wiley X   http://www.wileyx.com/
- Woolrich   https://www.woolrich.com/

Realistic Bug Out Bag

Medical:

- C-A-T   http://combattourniquet.com/
- HemCon   www.hemcon.com/
- H&H Medical   www.gohandh.com/
- North American Rescue
  http://www.narescue.com/

- Rescue Essentials
  http://www.rescue-essentials.com/

- Rusch, Inc.   www.ashermanchestseal.com/
- Sam Medical   www.sammedical.com/
- Water-Jel   www.waterjel.com/
- Z-Medica   www.z-medica.com/index.asp

Weapon:

- Beretta   http://www.berettausa.com/
- Colt   http://www.colt.com/
- Glock   http://www.glock.com/
- S&W   http://www.smith-wesson.com/
- Ruger   http://www.ruger.com/index.html
- Springfield Armory
    http://www.springfield-armory.com/

Realistic Bug Out Bag

Pets:

- American Humane Association
    http://www.americanhumane.org/
- ASPCA
    http://www.aspca.org/pet-care/animal-poison-control
- Center for Pet Safety
    http://centerforpetsafety.org/
- Cold Weather Pet Safety
    https://www.avma.org/public/PetCare/Pages/Cold-weather-pet-safety.aspx
- Healers   http://healerspetcare.com/
- Hurtta   http://www.hurtta.com/
- Kurgo   http://www.kurgostore.com/
- Kyjen   https://shop.kyjen.com/
- MTI   http://www.mtiadventurewear.com/
- North Coast Pets   http://www.northcoastpets.com/
- Pet Poison Helpline
    http://www.petpoisonhelpline.com/
- PowerBark   http://www.powerbark.com/
- Premier   http://www.petsafe.net/premier
- Ruffwear   http://www.ruffwear.com/
- ThunderShirt   http://www.thundershirt.com/

Miscellaneous:

- Stan's No Tube   http://www.notubes.com/

- Gorilla Duct Tape

    http://www.gorillatough.com/

- Ultimate Survival Technologies

    http://www.ultimatesurvival.com/

- Centers for Disease Control   http://www.cdc.gov/

- Federal Emergency Management Agency

    http://www.fema.gov/

- American Red Cross

    http://www.redcross.org/

References

[i] http://www.amazon.com/dp/B00HV4N78K/ref=wl_it_dp_o_pC_nS_ttl?_encoding=UTF8&colid=7H6CLRWJD4QR&coliid=I1FYQHO1UGDAGA
[ii] http://www.cdc.gov/parasites/crypto/
[iii] http://www.cdc.gov/parasites/crypto/treatment.html
[iv] http://www.cdc.gov/parasites/giardia/
[v] http://www.cdc.gov/parasites/giardia/treatment.html
[vi] http://www.cdc.gov/leptospirosis/
[vii] http://www.cdc.gov/leptospirosis/treatment/index.html
[viii] http://www.cdc.gov/healthywater/drinking/travel/backcountry_water_treatment.html
[ix] http://www.cdc.gov/healthywater/drinking/travel/emergency_disinfection.html
[x] http://hamexam.org/
[xi] http://www.amazon.com/Trauma-Care-Worst-Case-Scenario/dp/1495917517/ref=tmm_pap_title_0
[xii] http://www.amazon.com/dp/1496109511/ref=wl_it_dp_o_pd_nS_img?_encoding=UTF8&colid=7H6CLRWJD4QR&coliid=I1O5NEX6BYL2AE
[xiii] http://www.petpoisonhelpline.com/about/
[xiv] http://www.cdc.gov/healthywater/emergency/hygiene/index.html
[xv] http://www.cdc.gov/niosh/npptl/topics/respirators/disp_part/RespSource3basic.html

Made in the USA
Lexington, KY
24 September 2014